GENE A GEASLEN

INTO YOUR HANDS: MEMOIR AND WITNESS

"Grace always assumes positive intent"

Jerry Flora

INTO YOUR HANDS: MEMOIR AND WITNESS

Jerry Flora

Gracednotes Ministries

Gracednotes Ministries
425 East Walnut Street
Ashland, Ohio 44805

Into Your Hands: Memoir and Witness

Scripture is from the New Revised Standard Version Bible, copyright 1989, Division of Christian Education of the National Council of the Churches of Christ in the United States of America.
Used by permission. All rights reserved.

Printed in the United States

Copyright © 2015 Jerry Flora
All rights reserved.

ISBN- 13: 978-1516800049
ISBN- 10: 1516800044

To Julie,
whose middle name should be
Patience.

CONTENTS

Preface		1
Introduction		3
1	The Mystery of Duckling Number Two	9
2	Opportunity for Worship	13
3	Learning to Pray: One Story	16
4	How Much Bread Do You Have?	26
5	The Fragrance of Grace	29
6	Learning to Pray: Learning Love	32
7	A State of Tension	39
8	Called to Nothing Special	43
9	Open the Windows	46
10	Pursuing Adequacy: Thomas R. Kelly	52
11	Majesty and Mystery	59
12	Competent to Serve	62
13	Blow the Trumpet Softly	65
14	A Cause for Giving Thanks	67
15	Who Am I?	71
16	Practicing the Presence: Brother Lawrence	74
17	The World My Parish	80
18	A Cost to Consider, a Risk to Take	83
19	Mickey's Legacy	86
20	A Voice of Love	93
21	Revealing Divine Love: Julian of Norwich	96
22	Watch Out for Motorcycles	104
23	A Friend to Slaves	109
24	I Don't Get Anything Out of It	112
25	The Whole Story in Five Words	116
26	In the Hall of the Nursing Home	120
27	Last Days	122
28	Benediction	124

PREFACE

Books are never the work of one person alone. Writers always bring to their task who they are in personal experience, education, and work. That involves a host of people named and unnamed who touched their lives. These pages are the result of all that plus the encouragement of friends. Through the years a number of people have asked for something in print besides academic and ecclesiastical writing. Thus this little book of reflections on a journey.

First place among those who have contributed to it must go to my wife Julie, to whom it is dedicated, and to my spiritual director and friend, Dr. John Jorden. They know more about me than any other persons do. I can never thank them enough for their understanding.

Some of the reflections offered here were originally published in *the table*, the alumni magazine of Ashland Theological Seminary. They appear in reworked form with the permission of editors Eric Sandberg, Dawn Dever, and Glenn Black. Several fellow travelers have read and commented on parts of the manuscript, and I thank them for their generous help: Jason Barnhart, Laura Kollar, and Dr. Judy McLaughlin. "Last Days" was originally published in *Connexions*, the newsletter of the Epiphany Association in

Pittsburgh. It is reprinted here with the kind permission of the editor, Dr. Susan Muto.

Ashland author Dr. JoAnn Streeter Shade jump-started the project that resulted in this book, and I am grateful for her invaluable assistance in bringing it to completion. Finally, I wish I could thank all the friends who have encouraged me to get something into print, if only I could remember who you are. Hopefully these pages will reward your patience. God bless you all ways and always! Psalm 20:1-5.

INTRODUCTION

In the eighty-third year of my life I offer you these pages as a memoir and a witness. Both memoir and witness are fragmentary and scattered, far from complete. Since I can't divorce my faith from my life, the two are intertwined.

In life I am the eldest of three sons born to a pastor and his wife in the depths of the Great Depression. I am the husband of one wife, the father of two daughters, the grandfather of two young adults, and the recipient of blessed friendships. I am a Hoosier by birth and a Buckeye by adoption. Along the way I've had the privilege of living from coast to coast in the United States of America. Here is a map of the journey, a soft skeleton for the musings in this book:

Muncie, Indiana – birthplace and preschool years
Masontown, Pennsylvania – kindergarten and first grade
Elkhart, Indiana – second through seventh grades
Ashland, Ohio – middle school, high school, college, seminary, and marriage
Pasadena, California – advanced master's degree
New Paris, Indiana – pastor two years
Washington, D.C. – pastor seven years, birth of two daughters

Louisville, Kentucky – doctor's degree
Ashland, Ohio – professor thirty years, then retirement

As for faith, at age eight I walked the long red-carpeted aisle of our church, asked God to forgive my sins, confessed Jesus as his Son and my Savior, and invited him to live in my heart. With baptism a few weeks later I was now a registered Christian, a Jesus-follower. I received my faith first from my parents, then by formal instruction, and eventually in personal study. That does not mean the road has been smooth, straight, or boring. Pieces in these pages may suggest that questioning and doubt are part of my faith. As others have said, doubt is not really the opposite of faith. There is always a risk, a what-if in believing.

The real opposite of faith is certainty. Convinced believers may speak about a rest of faith or a certainty of faith. But without some evidence, some reason, some platform it may not be faith. It may be fideism, faith in faith. "My mind is made up. Don't confuse me with facts." A wise man commented that in all great religion there must be a reverent agnosticism.

I cannot prove to you by laboratory methods what I believe. I think there is sufficient evidence and reason for it. I hope my life is a witness to it. Witnesses and evidence can be examined and accepted or not. Even should Christianity not be true – even if there is no God – my faith has made me a better person. It helps me to see the glass of life half-full rather than half-empty. Without it, who knows where native self-centeredness would take me? Someone asked the Austrian-born genius Friedrich von Huegel why he was a Christian. The scholar replied, "Why, to save me from myself!" Exactly.

Few people in the past generation had the intellectual

power of Yale historian Jaroslav Pelikan. Having taught himself to read and type at age two, he went on to master Greek, Latin, and Croatian by ten. A doctorate at twenty-two and a dozen more languages prepared him for a lifetime of research in original sources. His long career led him to conclude, "If Christ is risen, nothing else matters. And if Christ is not risen – nothing else matters."

I have written those words inside the front cover of my Bible. They remind me of what started this way of living called Christian faith. I know of nothing but the Easter event that explains the explosion of courageous insight which marked the early mothers and fathers of the Way. They began with Jesus Christ risen, then bravely thought back to creation and forward to consummation.

Being a Christian, however, is more than just believing that something occurred. It's also "believing in," entrusting oneself to, betting one's life on the living Christ. As Brennan Manning put it, "I have not said in my heart, 'God exists,' until I have said, 'I trust you.'" He notes that Henri Nouwen wrote about forty books in which he often spoke about faith. But in his brief final work, *The Inner Voice of Love*, "faith" appears only once. "Trust" occurs sixty-five times. That is the true biblical idea of what it means to have faith, to believe. It is "Into your hands I commit my spirit. . . , O Lord, faithful God."

No solo act, however, this is a corporate experience as together with fellow believers we live in the world. Nouwen also spoke often about trapeze acts in the circus. A close friend of South Africa's Flying Rodleighs, he even practiced the first moves in flying. The Rodleighs told him that flyers, however daring their performance, are not the most important persons in the act. Instead, everything depends on the catcher. He grabs them to prevent them from falling, then flings them on to their next move. They literally hurl themselves into the hands of that partner. So also in this troupe called the church, the Christ who catches and holds and flings us forward is the most important. Consistently choosing to trust in him is the challenge.

One striking way of describing this comes from G. A. Studdert Kennedy. Serving as a British army chaplain in World War I, he was decorated for his acts of courage in combat under heavy gunfire. His faith was forged in battle. Here are lines selected from his poem "Faith."

> *How do I know that God is good? I don't.*
> *I gamble like a man, I bet my life*
> *Upon one side in life's great war. I must,*
> *I can't stand out. I must take sides. . . .*
> *How can you prove a victory before*
> *It's won? How can you prove a man who leads,*
> *To be a leader worth the following,*
> *Unless you follow to the death . . . ?*
> *I know not why the Evil,*
> *I know not why the Good, both mysteries*
> *Remain unsolved, and both insoluble. . . .*
> *I believe that Evil dies,*
> *And Good lives on, loves on, and conquers all . . .*
> *For God is love. Such is my Faith, and such*
> *My reasons for it. . . .*
> *It is a choice. I choose the Christ.*

I am profoundly grateful for the grace of choosing and being chosen. In the pages that follow I hope to convey to you something of that privilege. The reflections collected here were written at different times and for diverse reasons. All have been edited to appear in these pages. Sixty years of preaching and teaching have taught me it can be helpful to repeat what has been said. So you will find repetition as you read. Much more could be offered, and deserves to be mentioned. I can only invite you to share this handful of events in a blessed life together with musings sprouting from them. With only a minor change verses from Psalm 31 distill my journey:

> *Into your hands I commit my spirit;*
> *you have redeemed me,*
> *O Lord, faithful God. . . .*
> *I trust in you, O Lord;*
> *I say you are my God.*
> *My times are in your hand.*

All our times are in God's hand. The question is, what are we doing with that?

1

THE MYSTERY OF DUCKLING NUMBER TWO

One of the gems of my small city is its municipal park. It's actually two parks with a public golf course sandwiched between them. Together they contain softball diamonds, tennis courts, miniature golf, playground areas, picnic pavilions, basketball hoops, lawn bowling, horseshoes, a swimming pool, two ponds, and a band-shell with excellent acoustics and seating for 2,000 people. The ice cream stand is a favorite stop, as is the duck pond.

The pond is large enough that people fish there, and a flock of ducks is in residence year-round. Because my home used to be near the park, I have walked in it hundreds of times. Recently on a spectacular spring day I was walking there again, and I approached the pond. At its edge I saw a mother duck followed by seven ducklings marching in single file. The mother was leading her brood slowly along the edge of the pond just inches from the water.

I watched from a distance for she seemed to have

something intentional on her mind. Eventually she came to a spot where the ground sloped very near the water's edge, maybe only three inches above the water. From there she plopped easily into the pond followed at once by Duckling Number One.

Then it happened. Duckling Number Two did not follow. He or she stood stock still on the bank, unable or unwilling to jump. But why? Ducks are waterfowl. Water is their natural home. The jump was not far, no more than the duckling's height. Mother had gone in with scarcely a splash. Number One had followed, but Number Two was not budging. And Three, Four, Five, Six, and Seven were staying back in single file.

Mother swam quietly and slowly near the pond edge where the crisis was happening. Number One swam nearby, making circlets in the water. But Number Two would not, could not jump. Seconds ticked by, many seconds, a long time in duckling time. Then, with no warning or announcement, Number Two took the plunge. Immediately Three, Four, Five, Six, and Seven tumbled in.

What would stop a waterfowl from entering its true habitat, the water? Number Two did not even follow the example of its mother or sibling Number One. Not to enter one's true home is a mystery. What held that little bird back? Or what did it need to let go of?

My friend Clayton was a Mennonite bishop, which he said didn't amount to much. He was pastor to the pastors in a specified region of Pennsylvania. Clayton suffered much in his life, beginning at birth. His twin brother died when he saw the light of day while Clayton survived. That loss and its resulting survivor guilt mystified him throughout his life. He contracted polio and, although he recovered, it left him with a deformed leg. He could walk unassisted, but it required effort in a hippity-hop kind of gait.

In spite of suffering, Clayton lived with joy and grit. He earned a doctorate and became a well-known Mennonite educator. As the years passed he trained to become a spiritual director and was sought out for his wisdom and discernment.

When he came to Ohio to speak at a weekend retreat, I attended because I wanted to learn from him and be inspired by him. About three-fourths of the way through one of his presentations, he suddenly said, "Now, I want Jerry to come and finish this talk for me." I rose and stumbled through what I thought he might want to say. Unknown to any of us at the time, Clayton was ill, and it proved difficult for him to get through the retreat.

At one point he posed a question which has stuck in my mind for nearly thirty years. "What do you need to let go of for God to work through you?" It's a diagnostic question of the highest order. For, as evangelist D. L. Moody said long ago, the world has yet to see what one person totally committed to Jesus Christ can accomplish. Commitment involves letting go of the present in order to pursue a greater goal. It's like the trapeze flyer swinging out, letting go, then soaring to the hands of the catcher. But we hold back, we hesitate, we stand on the bank unable or unwilling to move. And we may be holding back others who, apart from us, are willing to jump in. I do it all the time.

My true home is God, the infinite eternal One before, behind, and between all things. I come from God, I belong to God, I return to God. That's the way it is meant to be. But I hesitate or refuse to live in such a way that I am embraced and nurtured in God, my true home. I procrastinate. I demur and delay at plunging into the vast illimitable Holy Love that overflows space and time.

As African American prophet Howard Thurman reportedly said, "There are whole tracts within me that have never yet heard the gospel." They desperately need good news. Really good news. "Lord, I believe. Help my unbelief!"

WHAT IS HOLDING ME BACK WHEN OTHERS ARE AWAITING MY DECISION SO THEY MIGHT FOLLOW?

2

OPPORTUNITY FOR WORSHIP

During my elementary school years our family worshiped in a carpeted sanctuary with divided chancel and stained-glass windows. Their symbols – lamb, book, key, hand, dove, wheat – intrigued and awed me. It was God's house, a holy place, and there must be no running or loud talk in there.

During high school I worshiped at summer church camp in morning watch and vespers by the lakeshore, chapel in the wooden tabernacle, and devotional campfires on the hillside. God was as close as the stunning stars – or the cute girl sitting nearby.

The college I attended had required chapel services, complete with a check of attendance. When I complained to a faculty member about the poor quality of those hours, he replied, "Whenever scripture is read and prayer is offered, there is opportunity for worship." So the ball was in my court to be attentive to what is, or at least might be.

Since then I have worshiped in Catholic, Orthodox, and Protestant settings, in cathedrals and campgrounds, in monasteries and mountains, at work as well as at home.

As Jesus said, worship isn't about place or time. God is spirit, and those who truly worship lift up their hearts to worship rightly. That is, no idol receives their praise. "We've always done it this way" can be an idol. "We have a new way to do it" can also be an idol. The truth is that we live in the present, where past and future touch, and the true god is the triune I AM. Or, in the words of Julian of Norwich, God is all-mighty Father, all-wise Son, all-good and loving Spirit. Worship is about that God, not me, not us.

Recently I inventoried the "choruses" of my youth. Some voiced praise; others, consecration. None of them, not one – so meaningful back then – is sung today. Yet the "contemporary" worship of that time, joined with stained-glass tradition, helped to grow this pilgrim.

Worship is about substance, not style. Yet substance must be expressed in some kind of style. Left to my own preferences . . . but it's not about my preferences, or me. It is about the Holy One who inhabits eternity, dwelling in light so dazzling it is darkness – the Mystery that causes both trembling and fascination. It is about the God who creates and also comes, the God who moves and yet remains, intimate but always unfathomed.

How shall we model that in our worship? The Eastern Orthodox tradition posits that worship is ongoing in heaven as saints and angels unceasingly adore the thrice-holy Trinity. An Orthodox worship service therefore intends to lift the congregation so all present can join in that unspeakable glory, then return to earth. To that end they engage all the senses using icons, incense, chanting, eucharistic elements, and various appropriate postures.

The heart of Christian worship is word and sacrament. The Word revealed, incarnate, and declared. Sacrament as rite and mystery and pledge of allegiance. These are worship's jewels. The question is, what kind of setting shall these jewels have? How can we best enhance their beauty?

The Hebrew scriptures suggest that at least some worship will be resplendent in pageantry worthy of a sovereign. It may resound with exuberant cheering. Some worship will be quietly contemplative, like a weaned child resting with its mother.

For all this we need the full counsel of God in holy writ. We need prayer informed by the communion of saints. We need the worship of lifting up and the worship of bowing down (Psalm 95). We need the anchor of history as well as the winds of the future. And we need to ponder the privilege that is ours. For whenever scripture is read and prayer is offered, there is opportunity for worship.

3

LEARNING TO PRAY: ONE STORY

My earliest memory of praying is rote prayer, bedtime prayer. Accompanied by Mother or Father, I knelt beside my bed to voice familiar words: "Now I lay me down to sleep; I pray the Lord my soul to keep." In our home we also spoke the second couplet: "If I should die before I wake, I pray the Lord my soul to take." Naming death at such an early age didn't seem to damage me or my brothers.

Following the rote prayer, we were allowed to add our personal wishes. Mine fell into a fixed pattern: "God, bless Mother and Daddy, Grandmother (who often lived with us), Guy and John (my brothers), and help me to be a good boy. Amen." That final clause was the hard part. It's not easy to be good when one has two younger brothers. Anything amiss must be their fault!

By age eight, I was a typical firstborn – usually responsible, sometimes disobedient, achievement-oriented, and lording everything over my siblings. One Sunday morning in church I responded to an invitation at the close of worship and walked down the long, carpeted aisle. I asked God to forgive me, invited Jesus to live in my heart, and waited for a soaking in baptism. The wait was several weeks until the great day came, and then I was a child of the King. But praying continued pretty much along the same lines as before: "God, bless . . . and help me to be a good boy."

In seventh grade I got a new Sunday school teacher. Sadly, I don't remember anyone who taught me at church until that time. I suspect the teachers were godly women whose influence, like pilings for a bridge, disappeared below the surface of my mind. Week after week Mr. Whybrew bore down on us boys with three topics.

First, he said, we should be witnessing for Christ by our words and our lives. Second, we should tithe our allowances and earnings from delivering newspapers, running errands, and mowing lawns. Third, to accomplish all this we needed to pray. And we didn't need to speak aloud, we could pray silently. That was a new idea, filling me with hope. Now I could pray before, during, and after math tests. (Please, God, make six times seven to be forty!)

By age sixteen I was ready to throw over most of it. Church and childhood praying lost their value as I struggled with doubt. My body was present in worship, but my mind was elsewhere. And melancholy did a number on my heart. I tried to become as hard as stone so I could never be hurt. Psychologists used to call adolescence the period of storm and stress, and rightly so. But two things held steady in my mind.

One was the stars. I was now the janitor at a local clothing store, working after school most of the year and full-time in summer. Our store closed at 5:30 but stayed open later on Saturday evenings. Some nights after getting home I walked to a large vacant lot away from the streetlights where I could gaze up and marvel at the display overhead. Ursa Major and Minor, Draco and Orion became familiar friends. King David, Alexander the Great, and Columbus all saw the same stars I did, and learned to journey by their direction. Could I?

Second, there was the Fourth Gospel's story of "doubting Thomas." He was so close to Jesus that when his teacher and friend began to move toward certain death, melancholy Thomas suggested that all the disciples should die with him (John 11:16). When Jesus was executed by crucifixion Thomas fixated on Jesus' suffering. The hands that healed the sick and blessed the children, the feet that brought good news had been smashed through with spikes. The side which housed his heart had been slashed open. It was a bloody, brutal death by public torture.

Thomas could not accept a wild story that anyone killed that way was alive – alive in a new, more powerful way. If he was to believe such a tale, he needed solid reasons. If he could see and examine evidence for Jesus' resurrection, then he would believe. So when the risen Christ appeared inside a locked room and confronted the apostle, he burst out, "My Lord and my God!" At sixteen, like Thomas, I wanted evidence. I needed assurance. I hoped for love.

Love came in the form of the blonde soprano in front of me in the high school choir. A year younger than I, she was my opposite in nearly every respect. The opposites attracted, and teenage romance began. As graduation approached a question surfaced. Would we, should we get married sometime down the road? Prayers for help were voiced, and the answer was no. (Billy Graham once said that if God had granted all his prayers in high school, he'd have married half a dozen girls before he graduated.)

Part of my no came from the interesting girls I met when I entered college. One brunette topped the list, and we soon became an item on our small campus. Instead of being opposites, Julie and I had much in common. Families of origin, religious experience, and interest in music were all similar. Our four-year courtship produced its questions, as you will see later, and there were many prayers about it. On the night before graduation a diamond ring appeared.

We married a year later on a humid, stormy afternoon. The winds blew and the heavens poured down rain. Large tree branches fell, lights flickered, and open windows crashed. People started for the church, then turned around and hurried home. But we were married.

Julie taught at Ashland's Pleasant Street School while I was a second-year student at Ashland Seminary. Professor Verno opened his classes with prayer, but his prayers sounded different from those I heard growing up. His prayers resonated with language from the Psalms. They echoed the Bible's own prayerbook, and I was intrigued.

After seminary graduation a different kind of intrigue took us down Route 66 to Pasadena, California, with meager savings in our pockets and worldly goods in our two-door Chevrolet. More about that later. Julie had a contract to teach in a private Christian school at half the salary of the public schools. At Fuller Seminary I began to work toward an advanced degree in biblical studies. One requirement was to pass an examination in a modern foreign language. I had studied ancient languages – Hebrew, Greek, and Latin – but no modern ones. So I began to teach myself German.

The exam itself was simple. My advisor, with two Ph.D.s, simply pulled a book written in German from his shelves. He picked a page seemingly at random, and told me to translate in the library for ninety minutes. Then he and another professor evaluated my work. I failed the exam, and was told I must retake the test. I failed again. (Can you really teach yourself German?) This time I got a letter stating that if it happened a third time, I must withdraw from the program. Weeks of desperate, intense study and prayer followed. "God, did you bring us 2,000 miles just for me to fail? I can't believe that. So help – please help!" And God did. I passed the German exam and went on to receive my graduate degree.

Nearly a decade of pastoral service followed in the 1960s, first in an Indiana village of one thousand and then in Washington, D.C. The village church had just experienced a split, so there was much to pray about. Then we discovered the lay leader and a young mother in the congregation were having an affair – more to pray about!

The church in the nation's capital needed to begin integration, but was losing members in the process – still more to pray about. And urban life could be dangerous, as we learned one hot September evening. With no air conditioning in the parsonage, we had the front door standing open to admit a little breeze. Suddenly two men barged in, faces covered and guns in hand. "Freeze!" they ordered. "Get on the floor!" We lay down like sticks of wood, but instantly feared for our two daughters asleep upstairs.

One guy held his gun on us while the other ransacked the house. We could hear drawers opening and our worldly goods falling to the floor. But what about Janet and Ann, ages five and one? When something like that happens, there's only one thing to do, and we did. We prayed. Silently. Desperately. Praying doesn't guarantee a happy outcome, but thankfully we were spared. The thieves took what little cash we had, tied us hand and foot, and left without waking our daughters. The pair continued their crime spree until they attempted a bank robbery, exchanged gunfire with the police, and were captured.

More study followed, this time in Louisville, Kentucky, where we attended a large Baptist church. We welcomed that opportunity because we had never experienced a really big congregation, and this one reportedly had 3,000 members. As we entered on our first Sunday I saw plates of bread and trays of cups on the table at the front. They were going to have a communion service. That could mean trouble.

Some Baptist churches have restricted participation in the Lord's Supper to congregational members only. Not knowing this church's protocol, I asked our usher, "Do you have open or closed communion?" The white-haired gentleman replied, "The pastor says that if you belong to Christ, all this belongs to you." We were home! That quiet layman had uttered a statement of profound theological and personal significance. For the next three years that church was our church.

Forty years old with doctorate in hand, I welcomed the invitation to return to my alma mater and join its faculty. Ashland Seminary's enrollment was increasing, the teaching load was heavy, and our daughters were beautiful girls. There was much to pray about, earnestly and gratefully. Then our family hit a rough patch that jolted all of us severely, and we went into counseling. I had leadership positions in our church, so I approached Pastor Arden and told him I wanted to resign. "I won't accept your resignation," he said. "We're a ministering congregation, and we are going to walk you through this." And they did. I learned how much loving support people can show through just a look in their eyes or a touch on the arm. During that time my prayers were a combination of "why?" and "help!" But one can't go on asking questions forever. The day came to sweep up broken pieces, put one foot in front of the other and walk with God into the future, whatever that might be.

Sometime in that period I learned to use a breath prayer, a short repeated phrase of six to eight syllables expressing the deepest wish of a person's heart. It's the prayer one could pray if unable to move or speak after a stroke. The most famous breath prayer is the one from Eastern Christianity called the Jesus Prayer: "Lord Jesus Christ, Son of God, have mercy on me." My breath prayer was "Lord, I would be wholly thine," and I prayed it for years. It proved especially helpful during long, questioning night-watches. I could repeat the sentence endlessly as prayer, or it could put me to sleep.

I also found it helpful in times of temptation and anxiety. "Lord, I would be wholly thine" could work for either situation. I could pray it for other people too, whether they knew it or not. My deepest wish for them, as for myself, was that they might be wholly God's. Because we lived about two miles from where I taught and I enjoyed walking home in late afternoon, the breath prayer became my marching song. It shortened to "Lord . . . thine. Lord . . . thine" – a steady rhythm that carried me easily to our little house and my waiting family.

Breath prayer came alive in a new way one evening as I met with friends of similar interest. We were part of an Order founded for the renewal of the church through spiritual disciplines. As the evening drew to a close, Harry offered a suggestion. He was a retired pastor, a former military chaplain. He'd lost his wife to cancer and volunteered with almost every worthy cause in our community. He delivered Meals on Wheels, built houses with Habitat for Humanity, transported shut-ins to the doctor, and seemed to know all the AIDS patients in town.

That evening Harry said, "I'd like us just to sit and pray in our hearts, 'Jesus, you are Lord. Jesus, you are Lord.'" So for some minutes we silently prayed Harry's prayer of adoration. During that time I became conscious of a change in myself. At first, I was praying with head reverently bowed, but when we finished my head was up and with a joyful heart I was murmuring, "Jesus, you are Lord! Jesus, you are Lord!"

Later I learned about centering prayer. It came through Catholic writers such as William Meninger, Thomas Keating, and Basil Pennington. It came through Mennonite friends Linda, Beulah, Joan, and Orthodox monk Father Michael. Centering prayer uses a single word repeated in silence to focus attention and maintain continuity while the heart moves toward God. Like breath prayer, centering prayer can include others as well as the self. At the outset I asked, "What about all the people I've promised to pray for and want to pray for?" The answer was, "Just bring them into the silence." Yes, God knows their needs better than I do. I can hold them in spirit, then release them into the loving light of the Holy One.

The slowly repeated word of centering prayer is intended to ultimately fall away in the stillness of contemplative prayer. There can the soul be like a weaned child, needing nothing but to rest with its mother (Ps. 131). In contemplative prayer we are simply with God, saying nothing, doing nothing, just being. Surely when Jesus spent whole nights in prayer, he wasn't talking all the time. Wrapped in silence, he was listening to his Father, resting in the heart of the Eternal.

I suspect that for us there may be a slow, natural progression here. Ideally we might go from a breath prayer in a short sentence, to the centering prayer of a single word, to the silence – however momentary – of resting in contemplative prayer. And likely with practice each stage of that will take years.

Most of the time, however, we need that centering word because, as Henri Nouwen said, our minds are like a banana tree full of monkeys. Darting and swinging, chattering and calling, our thoughts are constantly on the move. Voicing one word quietly and repeatedly can help to slow them down, calm them, and sometimes silence them. "Listen" or "holy" or "Jesus," spoken as often as needed, can usher one into the presence of the God who dwells in light eternal. There, if only for a moment, one can be with God in a way beyond all ways.

I've learned that prayerbooks can be helpful. Raised in the low-church tradition of extemporaneous praying, I need to go beyond whatever pops into my head at the moment. I need the continuity, the wisdom, the wealth of the greater church. I want to join the great river of prayer that has been flowing since the world began. So I employ sources for structured, ordered prayer among which the easiest to use is Phyllis Tickle's *The Divine Hours*. The prize for longest use, however, goes to *A Diary of Private Prayer*, by John Baillie.

Isn't something wrong here? Having begun in boyhood with rote bedtime prayer, am I now reverting to that? Or am I catching up with the power of repetition and the communion of saints? I think it's the latter, but there's still more to learn.

Set prayer and spontaneous prayer, liturgical prayer and informal prayer, prayer that is voiced and prayer that is silent – I want it all. I need it all. I am a beggar welcomed at the banquet of prayer, offered everything I wish from the feast spread before me. I am a child of the King, with instant access to the One who is eternally available. So many varieties, so many truths, so much beauty. I want and need the One who embraces it all. I need to be found in God, lost in God, used by God.

This is my story. There's more to say about learning to pray, and it will follow. What is here is fragmentary, incomplete, partial. But, like a finger angled at dusk toward the rising moon, it intends to point beyond itself. That's where the reality is.

4

HOW MUCH BREAD DO YOU HAVE?

The Middlebury Street of my Indiana boyhood was a fascinating place to live. The lazy Elkhart River flowed a couple blocks away, always inviting exploration. At a distance lay an open trash dump, full of material for building fragile forts. Across the way a symphony violinist opened his windows on warm summer evenings while he practiced. And every morning Mr. Anderson and his bulldog strolled up the street to open the corner service station.

Sometimes I was sent on a mission to Reuben's Grocery, source of all things edible. With bread in hand (9 cents per loaf), arrival at home meant the mission was accomplished. The mode of delivery – whether I bicycled, ran, or walked – was up to me.

Our Lord was sent into the world with a mission of his own. More than any other New Testament writing, the Fourth Gospel uses Greek words for "send." Most of the occurrences are about Jesus being "sent" by the Father. He was sent to proclaim liberty, to forgive, heal, and empower – to bring life to the full.

He in turn deputized the company of his followers, "As the Father has sent me, so I send you." "Very truly, I tell you, whoever receives one whom I send receives me; and whoever receives me receives him who sent me." For two millennia, his devout disciples have known that they are now sent in the extension of his mission. Beginning with the apostles, his pupils placard him before the world in deed and word. They do it corporately and individually. The mission is as vital as the sun for life and as variegated as the sun's rise. No two approaches seem to be the same.

Edith Margaret Clarkson was a young Canadian who fervently wanted to go abroad to offer the bread of life. But she lived in constant pain from migraine headaches and a damaged spine. No mission agency could risk sending her overseas. Jobs were scarce in Toronto's depressed economy, so she found work in northern Ontario. There she taught in a lumber camp and later in a mining area. In 1936, twenty-one years old and desperately alone, she wrote a poem that some say is the finest missionary hymn of recent years:

So send I you – to labor unrewarded,
To serve unpaid, unloved, unsought, unknown,
To bear rebuke, to suffer scorn and scoffing –
So send I you to toil for me alone.

Years later Miss Clarkson returned to Toronto, where she continued teaching and writing. In her long life she produced hundreds of poems, songs, articles, and seventeen books.

At age forty-eight, believing her early hymn was too

one-sided, she wrote a completely new version:

> *So send I you – by grace made strong to triumph*
> *O'er hosts of hell, o'er darkness, death and sin,*
> *My name to bear and in that name to conquer –*
> *So send I you, my victory to win.*

She said this way of thinking, "by grace made strong," is more biblical.

Despite lifelong suffering, Margaret Clarkson believed herself sent by her Master. Pupils in her classroom and readers in seven languages became her mission field. For her, as for John Wesley, the world was her parish. Her attention to opportunity opened the door.

Opportunities abound, but they also can overwhelm. The apostles, aghast at the size of hungry crowds, wanted to send them home. But Jesus asked, "How much bread do you have? Go and find out" (Mark 6:38 NLT). My late colleague Dr. Luke Keefer related that once preparing to preach, he despaired, feeling he had nothing to offer. Then he heard, "Just give me your loaves and fishes. I'll do the feeding."

Christ's followers are sent on mission in this world to bring the living Bread to malnourished multitudes. We give what we have, and Another does the feeding. Led by the Spirit, we choose the mode of delivery. Whether denominations, local assemblies, or individuals, our loaves and fishes can be multiplied by grace made strong. From all appearances the mission is indeed overwhelming. Again the question comes, "How much bread do you have? Go and find out."

5

THE FRAGRANCE OF GRACE

My career as a scientist lasted only minutes. Around age nine, nearsightedness demanded that I wear glasses. When I heard of an impending solar eclipse, I got an idea. Instead of trying to view the eclipse the usual way, through smoked glass, why not smoke up my glasses? With that kind of efficiency I could view the solar display hands-free.

The great day arrived, and I sped into action. With paper, twigs, and matches, I started a small fire outdoors. As the smoke curled upward, I grasped my glasses by the earpieces to hold them above the fire. Soon enough the lenses were turning smoky gray.

Then it happened. Without warning, the plastic frames sagged. They were starting to melt. I jerked the glasses away from the heat, which only hardened the now misshapen plastic. I didn't have my glasses anymore. I had a disaster.

There was nothing to do but stamp out the fire, creep indoors, and confess everything to my parents – well-known for their strict discipline. I braced myself for a thrashing or at least a severe tongue-lashing. To my astonishment, they graciously accepted my confession and arranged for new plastic to frame the much-needed lenses.

I cannot speculate on why my parents were so forgiving that day. I am simply grateful for their generous spirit. Who of us has not been surprised when treated better than we deserved? Words fail to describe such grace and mercy and compassion and understanding and magnanimity and generosity.

At times the Christian message has been framed as guilt, grace, and gratitude. In the best sense, generosity is an overflow of gratitude. But all too often my generous actions are based on external expectations, expectations voiced in terms such as ought, or must, or should. Being gracious then feels like a command. It has to be pumped up.

When I consider how abundantly I've been blessed, generosity comes easily. It is the outworking of grace bubbling up from inside. Those who have been forgiven much are able to love much. "Freely you have received," said Jesus, "freely give."

That includes giving others the benefit of the doubt, actively looking for what may be the best in them. Edwin Markham recast the Golden Rule in just four lines.

> *He drew a circle that shut me out—*
> *Heretic, rebel, a thing to flout.*
> *But Love and I had the wit to win:*
> *We drew a circle that took him in.*

Such largeness of spirit does not grow overnight. It takes years to mature. When it does, the fruit will appear naturally without being forced. It will possess the fragrance of grace.

Dr. Harold Kuhn was a noted scholar in the early years of the modern American evangelical movement. His academic discipline was philosophy, for which he prepared with a Ph.D. from Harvard. But he was no ivory tower scholar. Fluent in German, he and his wife worked every summer with refugees fleeing from Communist East Germany to freedom in the West. A committed Quaker, he modeled the integration of disciplined learning, deep piety, and devoted social service. Ashland welcomed him as a favorite guest speaker in both church and seminary settings.

While a student, I once was asked to drive him to the airport for his return flight home. En route I made some critical comments about a famous scholar's work. Dr. Kuhn listened quietly, then remarked, "Ah, but he is a great soul!" He knew the person behind the work. He knew the man, and his response had the fragrance of grace. Or, as James put it, "mercy triumphs over judgment."

To receive the grace of God and respond with gratitude can produce over time a generous, gracious spirit. Not our achievement, it is a divine work, beautiful and life-giving. "The fruit of the Spirit is . . . generosity" (Gal. 5:22).

My career as a scientist lasted only minutes. On the day of the sun's eclipse my parents' generosity overmatched my naive curiosity. When at last we can see the Son in all his glory, that will be the gift of grace. We won't need smoked glass.

1-1-16

6

LEARNING TO PRAY: LEARNING LOVE

When I was a boy, we always had Thanksgiving dinner at my grandparents' home. Although the trip to their house was roughly sixty miles, it seemed much, much farther. I was young, roads were only two lanes, World War II was on, and gasoline was rationed.

Every vehicle had an A, B, or C windshield sticker identifying how much fuel it was allowed to have. Printed on the back of the sticker, where everyone inside could see, were the words "Is this trip necessary?" Yes, it was, for Thanksgiving Day was our family reunion, and we saved gas for the trip.

My grandparents lived in a modest brown-shingle house in a tiny village in rural Indiana. To get there we had to leave the state route for a county road, then leave the county road for a township road. That finally brought us down the hill past the little white church into the village. It consisted of a handful of houses, a general store, the church, and a covered bridge.

My brothers and I clambered out of the car eager to see Grandfather and Grandmother again, and go exploring. But first there were hugs all round. Grandfather, a small, wiry man, hugged especially hard, unaware of his strength. Most women of that time wore leather oxfords, but Grandmother always wore cloth sneakers because she had painful arthritis in her feet.

Once everyone had commented on how much we boys had grown, we could go exploring. Behind the house was the garden, a small barn and barnyard, one cow to milk, a flock of chickens, and the chicken coop. At one corner of the house stood a rain barrel. If the level was low and you yelled down into it, you sounded like a very large person. Beyond the house and down a short path stood a small building that looked like a school-bus stop. It had a fingernail moon carved into the door, a wooden bench inside with a plate-size hole in it, and a mail-order catalog for leisurely reading.

Down the road stood the general store, and around the corner behind it was the covered bridge over the river. It was long as covered bridges go, braced with large timbers inside and underneath. If no cars were coming and you yelled into the bridge, you sounded again like a very large person. On the riverbank below the bridge lay plenty of flat stones good for skipping in the shallow river. With the right stone and a good throw, you might get more than three hops across the water.

But one didn't want to linger long, for Thanksgiving dinner would soon be ready. In rural Indiana, dinner meant the noonday meal. So it was back up the road to the brown-shingle house, which had an outstanding feature. Sunk partway into the lawn was a bathtub, and in the bathtub there were goldfish. The fish didn't like to be startled, but otherwise they seemed quite content with who they were and where they were. Occasional fresh water, plants to feed on, and cracker crumbs dropped from above made their life quite comfortable.

Cousins, nieces and nephews, aunts, uncles, and grandparents filled all available space inside the small house. The living room, dining room, and kitchen were a single L-shaped area. A potbellied stove stood in the crook of the L, and a hand pump brought water up from the well into the kitchen. Tables of different sizes now occupied most of the interior space.

When all were seated someone offered a prayer of thanks – thanks to God for the day, for safe travel, for time to be together, for our country, for those defending it, and for the food. The menu never changed. It was always fried chicken and everything to go with it – mashed potatoes, sweet potatoes, gravy, green beans, lima beans, corn in several forms, squash, tomatoes red and yellow, jellied salads, apple pie, cherry pie, mince pie, elderberry pie, and custard pie, all washed down with iced tea, hot coffee, and hand-pumped well water.

Cousins will be cousins anywhere, but at Thanksgiving dinner we tried to use our table manners. "May I have more mashed potatoes, please? Thank you."

"Uh-oh, I spilled some gravy. I'm sorry."

"Is there any more chicken? No drumsticks or white meat? What's left? Just neck, back, and gizzard? OK, may I have a gizzard, please?" I ate lots of gizzard.

With the meal finished, in the practice of that time the women and girls cleared the tables and washed the dishes while the men and boys moved outside. There was opportunity to check on the goldfish, yell down the rain barrel, pitch horseshoes, or visit the bus stop behind the house.

As the years went on, Grandfather couldn't walk outdoors very long, and needed to get back inside. There in the small living room he settled into his favorite chair, pulled his pipe from the bib of his overalls, and began to fill it. He stoked it and tamped it and lit it and drew on it until clouds of smoke arose, filling the room with the sweet aroma of Prince Albert pipe tobacco.

Some folks remained outdoors or in the kitchen, while others pulled up chairs in the living room to visit with Grandfather. His life had been a hard one, working as a small-time farmer and going bankrupt more than once. Because he farmed and logged with horses, many bones in his body had been broken from being kicked or stepped on. A barn accident had fractured his skull, so he wore a steel plate in his head. One finger was missing, and he had no teeth. A bushy mustache kept his mouth from looking sunken, and his eyes twinkled as he talked.

Grandfather liked to tell stories, stories about people he knew or had heard of. Stories about horses and mules he had worked with. Stories about his life with Grandmother since the day decades ago when he had a fistfight to win her for himself. He told stories about neighbors who worshiped in the white frame church on the hill above the village. Stories about folks who got what they deserved and folks blessed with more than they deserved. Stories about life's ironies, about love and justice, mercy and compassion. As he spoke, he often laughed until the tears came. But then his pipe went out. When that happened, he would pull out his red bandana, wipe his eyes, blow his nose, restoke the pipe, and start again.

Over the years my perception of Thanksgiving changed. At age six I was fascinated with the goldfish and the food. Ten years later I was trying to watch my table manners during dinner. With the passing of another decade I came to concentrate on the wiry little man who spoke of life and love, of suffering and solace. The goldfish were fun, the meal was monumental, but more and more I was learning love as I entered into the life of the one who – together with his Alta Ann – was the source of our family.

I've come to believe that learning to pray may take us through a process similar to that.

It begins with dissimilarity. Unlike goldfish, we humans are not fully at home in our environment. We are uneasy. Although we are creatures of time and space, those limits don't satisfy us. We wonder at what is, at sun and moon, stars and seasons, birth and death. We also wonder at what is not. And how did all this begin? What came before us? What lies beyond the horizon? Why is there anything at all? Why isn't there just eternal nothingness?

We are also puzzled by the mixed signals we get from the created world. The Himalaya Mountains and the Pacific Ocean are awe-inspiring to behold, breath-taking in their beauty. But in their fury they send avalanches and tsunamis crashing down, destroying everything and everyone in their path. The fish in the front lawn bathtub may be at home in their environment, but our human hearts strain at the limits confining us. We are confused by nature's beauty and barbarity. We seem to be made for something or somewhere or someone else. And prayer often begins in wonder, or dissatisfaction, or even desperation.

As we learn to pray, we use our table manners. "Please," "Thank you," and "I'm sorry" are necessary expressions which we never outgrow. Conversation may develop and wisdom, grief, or joy may be shared, but table manners are always needed. Other forms and experiences of prayer may arise. But if the teaching of Jesus is true, we will need to ask, say thank you, and apologize as long as we live. He encouraged it by what he said and how he lived, except that according to the record he never confessed a sin.

The real goal of all this praying, however, is to learn love. Just as a family gathers around the one who is its life-source, so in our praying we approach not a heavenly grandfather, but the One who inhabits eternity, the God who dwells in light unapproachable. Yet in Christ and by his Holy Spirit, the Spirit of Jesus himself, we who once felt outside now have access. We can come boldly, knowing that by grace we are accepted, included, welcome. We are members of the family, beloved children whose hearts cry, "Abba! Father!"

This is so deep, so tender and intimate that we cannot define it or analyze it. Like the children we really are, we can only experience it. The bond which "Abba" expresses contains all that we mean by love in its highest, deepest, most profound sense. This love will voluntarily go to a cross. It will lay down life not only for friends, but also for enemies. "God is love, and those who abide in love abide in God, and God abides in them. . . . There is no fear in love, but perfect love casts out fear. . . . We love because he first loved us" (1 John 4:16b, 18-19). Perfect love is mature love, love that has aged in adulthood, love that acts from itself rather than from some expectation, commandment, or duty.

This is the love St. Paul meant when he wrote, "Love is patient; love is kind; love is not envious or boastful or arrogant or rude. It does not insist on its own way; it is not irritable or resentful; it does not rejoice in wrongdoing, but rejoices in the truth. It bears all things, believes all things, hopes all things, endures all things" (1 Cor. 13:4-7). These words could be a picture of our Lord himself.

In his followers this is not childish love, puppy love, adolescent love, or self-centered love. This is the love of those who aren't even conscious of loving because they have practiced until it has become second nature to them. It is learned love, skilled love, mature love, divine love in human life.

But how do we learn this love? We abide, we remain. We make our home, we build our nest, we sink down into God. As the family gathered around Grandfather, so we draw near to God. The real purpose isn't to learn or even listen – it's just to be close and savor the presence of the One whom Lady Julian called all-powerful, all-wise, all-loving and good. That threefold energy, that triune life, that infinite joy, is the goal we seek.

Learning to pray is learning to move from the gifts to the Giver, knowing we will always need to say please, thank you, and I'm sorry. Beyond that, as Teresa of Avila pointedly put it, "The important thing is . . . to love much; do, then, whatever most arouses you to love."

7

A STATE OF TENSION

World War II began in the month I started first grade. Two years later, in December 1941, the United States entered the conflict. Together with my classmates, I saved money to buy war bonds, collected metal cans for recycling, and filled potato sacks with milkweed pods for use in life jackets.

Sometime in those years Rice Elementary School sponsored a fund-raising carnival. One of the booths featured a dart game. The targets were pictures of faces, faces of the enemy – Germany's Adolf Hitler and Hideki Tojo of Japan. But I was in tension. Hurling pointed darts at human faces, even their pictures, didn't seem right to me. The war was being personalized.

American Civil War general William Tecumseh Sherman famously said, "War is hell." One month after that conflict ended he wrote, "I confess, without shame, that I am sick and tired of fighting. . . . [I]t is only those who have never heard . . . the shrieks and groans of the wounded and lacerated . . . that cry aloud for more blood, more vengeance,

39

more desolation." For Sherman, war was personal.

Eighty years later, the advent of nuclear weapons exponentially multiplied Sherman's comment. When the first atomic bomb was tested in the New Mexico desert, project director J. Robert Oppenheimer quoted from the Bhagavad Gita, "Now I am become Death, the destroyer of worlds." War had become impersonal. Enemies would no longer be killed, they would be neutralized.

Howard Thurman, spiritual advisor to Martin Luther King, Jr., wrote, "War and the threat of war has covered us with heavy shadows. We do not know how to do what we know to do. We do not know how to be what we know to be." Or, as Dr. King put it, "Many men cry Peace! Peace! but they refuse to do the things that make for peace." Often we feel like the Hebrew poet who lamented, "Too long have I had my dwelling among those who hate peace. I am for peace; but when I speak, they are for war" (Ps. 120:6-7). We find ourselves in a state of tension.

What can we do? Where do we begin? For Christians, one angle of approach – not the only one – is to start with ourselves. In the month World War II ended, I entered seventh grade in Roosevelt Junior High. With no cafeteria or lunchroom, we who could not get home at noon carried our lunches to school. We ate in a large study hall at individual desks screwed to the floor in straight rows.

A hulking ninth-grader often taunted me by raiding my lunch. When the monitor on duty was not looking, he would sneak behind me and snatch whatever he could. He wasn't hungry, he just enjoyed this form of bullying. I tried carrying extra food in my lunch to offer him. But nothing seemed to help. He simply enjoyed the taunting game.

One day I spotted him tiptoeing toward me again. I

stood up. Just as he reached for my lunch, I hit him in the jaw with a right hook. It was a spontaneous, unplanned preemptive strike. A startled expression crossed his face, and he silently slunk back to his seat. He never grabbed at my food again. For the remainder of the school year I tried going out of my way to be kind to him, and by year's end we were beginning to warm to each other.

You may applaud my action, or you may wince at it. Our conflict was petty and personal. On a much larger scale, what about nations that bully other nations? Or acts of intentional aggression? Or cruelty for cruelty's sake?

In his story of the wheat and weeds, Jesus may have implied that the world can grow better and worse at the same time. Wheat and tares grow together until the harvest. Wars and rumors of war accompany the good news of the Kingdom. He also challenged listeners to resist evil creatively, to do the unthinkable – love their enemies. St. Paul, applying the news of Christ now risen, wrote to the Corinthians at their double address "in Corinth" and "in Christ" (1 Cor. 1:2). That dual residence, that dual allegiance, is the tension which marks all followers of Jesus in this age. We are in the world but not of it. The issues are complex and the implications diverse.

Ancient wisdom says, "Be not angry that you cannot make others as you wish them to be, since you cannot make yourself as you wish to be" (Thomas à Kempis). So I must begin by confessing my personal pride, personal greed, fear, anger, and indifference – and then the sins of my fellow believers.

I pray with Harry Emerson Fosdick:

*Lo! the hosts of evil round us
Scorn your Christ, assail his ways! . . .
Grant us wisdom, grant us courage
For the living of these days.*

*Heal your children's warring madness,
Bend our pride to your control;
Shame our wanton, selfish gladness,
Rich in things and poor in soul. . . .*

*Save us from weak resignation
To the evils we deplore . . .
Grant us wisdom, grant us courage,
Serving you whom we adore.*

The praying continues and so it must, as personally as possible. The tension also continues.

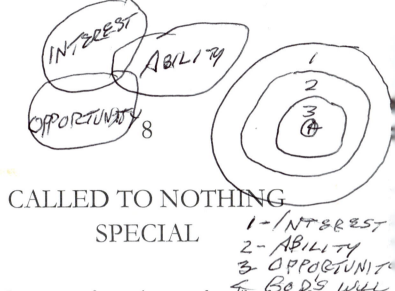

CALLED TO NOTHING SPECIAL

I spent part of my early years a few miles from Notre Dame University. The Fighting Irish have always had one of the nation's best college football teams. Led in those days by coach Frank Leahy, they overwhelmed most opponents. Although I enjoyed vacant lot football, I wasn't cut out to be a football player. Skinny, awkward, and nearsighted, I had interest but lacked ability.

In sixth grade I tried out for the Rice Elementary School track team, but I wasn't fast enough to win any races. Again, I had interest but not ability. (Doris, who lived up the street, could outrun any boy in the neighborhood.) It fell to one of my brothers to be a runner and successful track coach.

Many years later I heard a speaker say that discerning God's call involves both interest and ability, and also opportunity. The three, he said, are like concentric circles. Each is smaller than the one before, moving toward the center of God's will.

When people feel called to some kind of Christian service small or large, they have interest in helping others. They want to bring God's saving truth and healing love into others' lives. They hope to make a difference in the world. But if that call is truly from God, it will likely feel overwhelming. The task is too big, our abilities too small.

No biblical prophets volunteered for their mission. Moses knew he was not eloquent. Deborah was drafted by the insecure Barak. Amos belonged to no prophetic guild or family. Jeremiah protested that he was too young. ==One mark of a genuine call, you see, is that it seems impossible==. The task is too ==big, our abilities too small.==

If, however, we believe it is truly God calling, we will join Isaiah in the risk of faith to say, "Here am I; send me!" Interest may need to be focused, abilities must be honed, and we watch for doors of opportunity to open. Or, as Hebrew prophets often had to do, we may knock at doors that are barred shut. And sometimes we realize the call isn't to what we thought it was.

Scotsman Oswald Chambers refocused what the call looks like. Artistically gifted, he earned a master's certificate from the National Art Training School and a degree in art from the University of Edinburgh. But he felt a call to Christian ministry, trained for it, then taught in the U.S. and Japan. He married Gertrude (Biddy) Hobbs, a high-speed shorthand expert. Together they started a small school in London to teach students bound for the mission field.

When World War I broke out, they closed the school and became missionaries themselves. Their assignment was a British army camp in Egypt near the pyramids of Giza. The intense heat and strenuous service weakened Chambers so that when he contracted appendicitis, complications from it quickly killed him. Biddy continued to work among the troops, then returned to London. There she transcribed her shorthand notes from Oswald's messages. With them she created the world's most famous book of daily readings, *My Utmost for His Highest*.

Speaking to his missionary recruits, Chambers said, "We make calls out of our own spiritual consecration, but when we get right with God He brushes all these aside, and rivets us with . . . being made broken bread and poured-out wine. God can never make us wine if we object to the fingers He uses to crush us with" (Sept. 30).

"God plants His saints in the most useless places. We say – God intends me to be here because I am so useful. . . . God puts His saints where they will glorify Him, and we are no judges at all of where that is" (Aug. 10).

"You are expecting God to tell you to do a big thing, and all He tells you to do is to 'come'" (Oct. 8). "No Christian has a special work to do . . . Our Lord calls to no special work: He calls to Himself" (Oct. 16).

More basic than any call to service is the call to discipleship. That primary call is simply to come. "Follow me" – an obedient, disciplined, transforming relationship with the living God.

Our calling can seem, at least at times, to be a gift. But life in Christ is intended to move us beyond any gift to the Giver. It's the pilgrim journey of following, bonding, and likeness.

We can indeed discern God's call to service through interest, ability, and opportunity. But the ultimate call is to "know you, the only true God, and Jesus Christ whom you have sent" (John 17:3). That is both center and circumference, prologue and pathway. Anything more is commentary.

9

OPEN THE WINDOWS

During my high school years our church had midweek prayer and Bible study. Sometimes there was more study than praying, and more than once the prayer requests took so long there was only time for a benediction. We had to conclude on time because choir practice followed immediately afterward.

I don't recall much from those sessions except that a few friends and I used to attend. The meetings were not memorable, but I do recall the night Dr. Wiley prayed. He had retired from teaching mathematics at one college, and our local college asked him to teach here. He was a quiet, dignified, white-haired Quaker, and I can only suppose he was a good instructor. But I will never forget the night Dr. Wiley prayed.

At some point during the season of prayer, as it was called, I heard his gentle voice. "O God," he said, "open the windows of our souls." For years I had heard prayers at home and in church, but I'd never heard anyone pray like that. "Lord," he repeated, "open the windows of our souls." He prayed on for a few sentences, then concluded, "Open the windows of our souls."

Those words, that image, marked me forever. To think of my soul as a house with windows closed or shuttered to the light of heaven – that was a troubling thought. But the idea that I could ask God to open those windows was liberating. I was never quite the same after the night I heard Dr. Wiley pray.

Some years later, when Julie and I had been married a short time, we moved to Pasadena, California. Our plan was for me to attend graduate school while she taught in the elementary grades. There were other reasons for moving too. We were responding to the lure of sun and warmth, and the chance to escape our small-town Midwestern upbringing.

We found a congenial church and soon became part of its active life. I enjoyed watching the pastor and his wife lead the congregation together. They were an older couple approaching retirement. Paul was a pleasant, active shepherd of the flock, and Florence kept him organized. Everything he needed to know was in the little black notebook she always carried. I chuckled at how often she made entries in it or consulted what she already had written.

Florence was wiser than I knew, and I learned from her and Paul. Sometime in the two years we spent with them I heard her quote a poem whose author is unknown:

> *Every morning lean thine arms awhile*
> *upon the windowsill of heaven*
> *and gaze upon thy Lord.*
> *Then, with the vision in thy heart,*
> *turn strong to meet thy day.*

To lean, to look over into the eternal world and linger there – how inviting! How encouraging, especially if it can govern the rest of the day. I can lean on a fencepost if I'm contemplating the pasture beyond. And I can lean on heaven's windowsill if I'm commencing another day.

Windows allow light and air to enter, bright light and fresh air. Windows also keep out dirt, noise, storms, and unwelcome flying things. Windows give access or deny it. If heaven has a windowsill, I can lean there awhile before diving into the tasks of my day. When Dr. Wiley prayed, "O God, open the windows of our souls," he left it at that. Just what windows we open and what scenes we view are up to us.

There are various windows to God available to us such as the created world, the written word, and the living Word, Jesus Christ. I like to apply this image to the window of the created world available to the senses. Maltbie Babcock, an outstanding athlete at Syracuse University, went on to become a popular pastor in Baltimore and New York City. Handsome, vigorous, and personable, Babcock attracted people wherever he went. Before his tragic early death he wrote these lines:

This is my Father's world, and to my listening ears
All nature sings, and round me rings the music of the spheres.
This is my Father's world: I rest me in the thought
Of rocks and trees, of skies and seas –
His hand the wonders wrought.

Babcock loved to run before running became popular. His first pastorate was near Lake Ontario, and he often ran two miles in early morning to the top of a hill. There, he could see "my Father's world." For him the creation was not some impersonal entity existing of its own accord. It was, rather, the handiwork of the personal God whose energy is love. That's why, to listening ears, "all nature sings." That's why rocks and trees, skies and seas, are not "natural" — they are wonders.

Early Celtic Christians felt the same way. The Romans never managed to conquer Scotland and Ireland. They were never part of the Roman Empire. So for several centuries Christianity flourished there without the top-down style typical of the Western church. Theirs was a rural faith which gave special attention to sun and moon, stars and seasons.

Celts developed prayers for all their daily activities. Greeting the sunrise, getting dressed, building the fire, cooking and eating, working in the fields, weaving cloth, catching fish, milking the cows, banking the fire at night — nothing was too trivial for prayer. The form was highly trinitarian as they invoked Father, Son, and Spirit along with angels, saints, and holy mother Mary.

Leaning on heaven's windowsill each morning gives light and life to the day. What we see in the world depends in part on where and when, how and why we look. Many believers will say that in creation they see order and beauty, and feel resulting wonder. The majesty of mountains, the crash of surf, and the kiss of sunset all declare the wonder of the God who creates. It's just as possible, however, to look at nature and see ugliness, savagery, and chaos. Mountains produce avalanches, surf can turn to tsunami. Everything that lives, lives on the death of something else. Herbivores kill grasses in order to survive, and carnivores kill herbivores. Nature is indeed "red in tooth and claw" as well as wonder-full.

One summer while my wife and I were living in California we camped in Yosemite National Park. It wasn't because we are great campers or chose that for our vacation. We were temporarily homeless. We were between apartments, having learned too late that what was promised to us was not yet available. So we house-sat for one couple while they traveled east on vacation. Then we house-sat for our pastor and his wife (the one with the little black notebook) while they camped in Yosemite. They offered to leave their tent up so we could use it until our apartment was ready. Thus for ten days and nights we camped on the floor of Yosemite Valley, that spectacular, jaw-dropping gash in the earth's crust.

The cliffs surrounding us were so high it was mid-morning before we could see the sun. Filtering softly through the trees, it created waves of light streaming toward us. El Capitan, Half Dome, and other rock formations towered a half-mile above our heads. The sequoia and redwood trees were more than gigantic. Some were as tall as a football field standing on end. One of the oldest first saw the light of day about the time Abraham left Ur to migrate to the land that God would show him. And in the high back country nestled dozens of tiny lakes, diamonds sparkling in the sunlight, awaiting discovery.

Harden Lake was one of those. The trail from the highway wound through long-needle pines which carpeted the ground and perfumed the air. After about a half-mile it opened out to the lake itself, a glistening dewdrop welcoming its visitors. We could see two or three people on the opposite side, but apart from them we had it all to ourselves. Warm morning sun, clear mountain air, and spring-fed lake combined in a beauty beyond words. Time stopped as we savored the scene's incredible beauty. Together we walked and sat, splashed and basked. It was Eden. It was heaven.

Such experiences are gifts not often repeated. But each day brings its own gifts if only we open the windows of our soul to notice. Doubtless Dr. Wiley had more than this in mind when he prayed. Still, so much of what is called spiritual formation needs to begin not with prayer techniques or heady devotions, but externally. Honoring the body, attending to the senses, being alert to the created world – we need to start there. Hebrew psalmists, Augustine in his *Confessions*, and Francis of Assisi all wrote about taste and touch, sight and sound in our life with God. And Jesus called attention to wildflowers, small birds, and a Father who cares for them and even more for us.

Maltbie Babcock wrote to praise God for the external world. Florence's poem turned inward in its attention to our Lord. Dr. Wiley didn't specify what he meant by opening the windows of our souls. I do want my soul to be open – open to the creation and the creator, thanking God and attending to God's world. Holy Spirit, please make that happen today and every day!

10

PURSUING ADEQUACY: THOMAS R. KELLY

I first heard of *A Testament of Devotion* while I was a student in college. It's a book from an Ohio-born Quaker, Thomas R. Kelly, and Sylvia recommended it. She had served as a missionary in China until the Communist takeover forced her and her husband to return to the States. Here she became a guidance counselor in one of the school systems near Ashland. An invited speaker at Christian events, she often dwelt on topics such as obedience, contemplation, and suffering.

Sylvia recommended Kelly's book to her hearers, and so I tried to read it. But I didn't like it. The language seemed strange, for my conservative Protestant background didn't describe God as the Center or the Seed or the Abyss. Sure that Kelly at times was mistaken, I jotted in the margins a Bible reference or two where I thought he was wrong. I laid the book aside, later read some more, laid it aside again, and read still more. Despite my misgivings, I finished the book in a couple of years. By that time I was intrigued, hooked, and

I've been reading it ever since. It is the longest-standing devotional help in my life, which I've read at least twenty times. Douglas Steere, the book's editor, wrote, "The story of Thomas Kelly's life is the story of a passionate and determined quest for adequacy." I could identify with that because I wanted my life to be adequate too. Here is the story.

Thomas Kelly's journey began on a farm near Chillicothe, Ohio, where he was born in 1893 to devout Quaker parents. Tom was just four years old when his father died. His mother wanted her children to receive a good education, so she moved the family to Wilmington, Ohio, where Quakers had started a small college. There Kelly majored in chemistry, delighted to discover the world of hard facts and scientific knowledge. He also indulged his penchant for pranks, such as riding his motorcycle across the campus at breakneck speed.

After graduation he went to Haverford College in Philadelphia, the elite among Quaker schools, for further study in chemistry. There on his first day he met the famed philosopher Rufus Jones. In his excitement he said to Dr. Jones, "I am just going to make my life a miracle!" Neither of them could have imagined what that might mean.

Kelly's enthusiasm carried him the next year to Canada where he taught science, but a drive for more learning drew him back to the States. World War I intervened, and in the best Quaker fashion he volunteered to serve wherever needed. He spent nearly a year working in England with German prisoners, the beginning of what became a longstanding concern for the people of Germany.

Back home he entered Hartford Theological Seminary, graduating in 1919. The next day he married his fiancée Lael Macy, then returned to Wilmington College where he taught Bible. Two years of that and his restless ambition drove him back to Hartford to begin Ph.D. studies in philosophy, which he completed in 1924. He not only received his degree but also was elected to the prestigious honors society Phi Beta Kappa.

Quaker leaders in America then asked Dr. and Mrs. Kelly to go to Europe and work with their relief centers in Berlin and Vienna. The goal was to lead them in becoming hubs of Quaker study and service for all who might be interested. Tom's intellectual ability, familiarity with Quaker life, deep spirituality, and his fluency in the German language combined to make him the ideal choice for the delicate job.

The Kellys returned from Germany in 1925, locating in Richmond, Indiana, where he began to teach philosophy at Earlham College. Now thirty-two years of age, he was convinced that hard-nosed academic life was his true calling. His earlier joy with chemistry echoed in the all-out passion with which he approached philosophy. Despite that, students found him interesting, approachable, and full of much good humor. After five years Kelly moved his wife and their two year-old daughter to Massachusetts in further pursuit of his passion for academic achievement.

He wanted most of all to become a world-class scholar, which in his mind meant a Ph.D. in philosophy from Harvard University. He already possessed the degree from Hartford with Phi Beta Kappa honors, but that was not enough. With little precedent for anyone seeking a second doctorate in the same field, Harvard reluctantly admitted him to begin study which he finally completed in 1937. Research would have to be piecemeal, for along the way he taught at Wellesley College in Massachusetts, again in Indiana at Earlham, and then at the University of Hawaii.

At the latter school he was able to interact with Asian scholars and study Eastern philosophies in his quest for world-class knowledge. A son was born into the family, so the Kellys were now a family of four. But funds were scarce and borrowed, and Tom's health was often threatened. He experienced severe hay fever, kidney stone attacks, sinus infection requiring surgery, and "nervous exhaustion," all of which rendered him bedfast at times.

Fortune smiled at last in 1936 when Haverford College invited him to join their faculty. His colleague in philosophy would be Douglas Steere, eventually perhaps the century's most famous American Quaker. Kelly moved quickly to complete the research for his Harvard doctorate, wrote his dissertation, and it was published to good reviews. In the autumn of 1937 he traveled to Massachusetts for the final step, the oral defense of his new dissertation. There he lived out the nightmare of every doctoral candidate. In the stress of the examination his mind went blank.

He could recall nothing of what he had studied, or learned, or written. This had happened years before when he finished his first Ph.D. Back then the Hartford examiners had sympathized, encouraged him, and he recovered to give a brilliant defense of his research. But the Harvard committee was not so sympathetic. They failed him on the examination and, drawing on the unusual circumstances of his admission, they told him he could never have a second chance.

He returned to Philadelphia defeated, despondent, and possibly – his wife feared – suicidal. He had failed himself, his family, and his calling. It had all been for nothing. All the moves, all the family disruption, the years of study, sacrifice, indebtedness, and broken health – it was for nothing.

When her husband arrived home that evening, Lael

Kelly quickly called for Douglas Steere and the college president to come to the house. They reminded Tom that he already had a Ph.D. in philosophy, assured him that his job was not in jeopardy, and promised there would be no announcement of what had happened. In the weeks that followed Steere walked with Kelly through his dark night of grief. More than anyone except Lael Kelly, Douglas Steere knew Thomas Kelly's despair.

Then, as Steere described it, "No one knows exactly what happened, but a strained period in his life was over. He moved toward adequacy. A fissure in him seemed to close, cliffs caved in and filled up a chasm, and what was divided grew together within him." He spoke and wrote with "the same voice, the same pen, the same rich imagery that always crowded his writing, and on the whole a remarkably similar set of religious ideas. But now he seemed to be expounding less as one possessed of '*knowledge about*' and more as one who had had unmistakable '*acquaintance with.*'"

As Kelly resumed his usual life word spread about the authenticity, freshness, and power of what he had to say. Quaker groups invited him to speak, and their magazines welcomed his articles and essays. The American Friends Service Committee asked him to go once more to Germany in the summer of 1938, for it seemed clear the Nazi government would soon seal the borders. Away from his family he traveled for weeks visiting Quaker groups, speaking when asked, listening and encouraging as much as possible. While there he met a young rabbi named Abraham Joshua Heschel, destined for later fame.

Deeply moved by the injustice and suffering he saw, Kelly knelt to pray in the great cathedral at Cologne. There he felt God laid the burden of the entire world on him, then assured him that with divine help it could be borne. Kelly would later say that God doesn't want us to carry the whole world, but only what has been personally assigned to us. "We cannot die on *every* cross, nor are we expected to."

He returned from Germany in September, the last passenger to leave the steamship. In the weeks that followed he often said to his friends, "I have been literally melted down by the love of God." He wrote to Rufus Jones, now his mentor, "I have longed to talk about *Him* who deals so tenderly and lovingly to undeserving hearts."

That sense of human undeserving, divine grace, and the spontaneous response of grateful love marked his life for the next three years. He had found the adequacy that he pursued so long, but it was a divine gift rather than the fruit of his quest. Now he taught, preached, and wrote from a spiritual reality few people could fathom. For two decades he had experienced drivenness, distraction, and depression. Now he was – to everyone's amazement – integrated and whole, simplified, loving, and joyful. Colleagues respected him, his church trusted him, and his two young children adored him.

A small group of college students began meeting with him to read spiritual classics, discuss their meaning, and prepare to move out into lives of worshipful service. Dr. Kelly himself lived more fully than ever, relishing family and friends. Vacations in Maine, building toys for his children, and his boyish humor were special delights. He continued to teach, speak, and write for Quakers beyond Philadelphia until January 17, 1941. That evening while drying the dinner dishes he experienced a fatal heart attack, and then he was gone.

When Kelly died, his colleague Douglas Steere was on sabbatical leave. He cut it in half in order to substitute in his friend's classes and sift through the essays, articles, and lectures Kelly had left behind. From them he quickly selected five, wrote a biographical memoir, and titled the collection *A Testament of Devotion*. It was a testament to God's amazing grace, Kelly's devotion to God, and his calling as a committed follower of Christ. As Kelly wrote, "Continuously renewed immediacy, not receding memory of the Divine Touch, lies at the base of religious living. . . . Religion as a dull habit is not that for which Christ lived and died."

Although Kelly said almost nothing about himself in its pages, the note of personal experience in the book is strong. Readers quickly learn they can find themselves in its 100 pages. The final essay, "The Simplification of Life," concludes with a reference to death. Otherwise its contents would place it first, to be followed by the other chapters on prayer, obedience, community, and social concern. His counsel on humility and holiness, simplicity and suffering reads as if it were written today. Harper and Brothers published the book in 1941, and it has never gone out of print. The current edition contains an introduction by Richard Foster who tells how Kelly's book empowered a pivotal decision in his life.

Some reviewers have described this as among the finest devotional writing of the twentieth century. Some readers take it in small doses, just one or two pages a day, then begin again when they finish. For over a half-century the book has been my companion. While the final entry is titled "The Simplification of Life," the essay speaks powerfully about the *integration* of life. It addresses all who feel driven and pressured, divided and weakened by their many concerns. It offers gentle wisdom about God's healing of our spirits so we become whole, complete, integrated human beings. It reminds me to trust the One who said his yoke is easy and his burden is light.

11

MAJESTY AND MYSTERY

US Highway 20 stretches between the Atlantic and Pacific oceans, passing north of Ashland on its way. When I used to visit my fiancée before we married, I often drove the section of that road between Norwalk and Fremont, Ohio. It was, and is, an easy ride on a four-lane divided highway through level farm country and small towns.

Easy, that is, until you come to Clyde (pop. 6080). In that town traffic signals, six of them now, bisect the four-lane highway at uneven intervals. Driving then becomes a challenge of stop-and-go or finding an unposted speed at which one can sail through all six stoplights.

Returning home late at night, I prayed more than once, "Lord, if all the lights in Clyde are green, does that signal your blessing on our marriage?" Stoplights or not, Julie and I are closing in on our 60th wedding anniversary.

I am not the first person to pray for a green light or a parking space. But discerning writers have said that before we think about how to pray, we should consider the God we pray to. As Julian of Norwich put it, "The whole reason why we pray is summed up in the sight and vision of him to whom we pray."

The God whom Jesus called Abba is "the Father almighty, maker of heaven and earth." When I gaze at the night sky, I am awed at the creator I so lightly call God. The Milky Way soars overhead with its 200-400 billion stars, about fifty billion of which have their own planets. Hurtling through space, the galaxy clocks somewhere around 30 million miles every day. And ours is only one of an estimated 200 billion galaxies in the observable universe. Then I remember that up until a hundred years ago people thought the Milky Way was the entire universe.

It is important, even imperative for me to keep that in mind. The God whom I worship, to whom I pray, is the vast, illimitable Mystery behind, before, and within all creation. But, as another has said, this God also stoops and stays. Or, in the words of African-American poet James Weldon Johnson in *God's Trombones*,

> *This Great God,*
> *Like a mammy bending over her baby,*
> *Kneeled down in the dust*
> *Toiling over a lump of clay*
> *Till he shaped it in his own image;*
> *Then into it he blew the breath of life,*
> *And man became a living soul.*

Holy and awesome is the three-personed God who will stoop to create and then invite the creature to share the love that causes creation. In Jesus, the second person stoops still further and becomes an earthling. For a human lifetime he wills to obey the Father and pours himself out all the way to a sacrificial death, in an act of infinite agape-love. Now exalted, he stays with us in the person of his own Spirit, not only with us but also in us, to pray in ways beyond our own.

"This Great God" is Abba, the Father to whom we infants in the universe babble our praise. This God is the King, the saving Lord whose stooping we honor in worship and service. This God is the Spirit, the holy empowering, guiding, mothering, protecting Friend who engages all the details of our little lives, now enlarged because of infinite love.

It was twelve years into our marriage when Julie and I were robbed in our parsonage home. The encounter took place so quietly that our daughters slept through the whole thing. Our five-year old only learned of it days later from a neighborhood playmate. The sense of invasion, violation, and helplessness lingered long afterward. The bold thieves who walked in on us assaulted other victims and even returned to our neighborhood. They repeated their caper more than a dozen times in greater Washington, D.C., before they were captured.

Why were we spared that night? My only explanation is to say that God is great and God is good. Beyond that I cannot go. Questions remain, many questions, much more pressing than traffic lights or parking spots or personal safety. But I dare not forget the majesty and mystery of the One to whom I pray. I dare not dumb down the God Julian called all-mighty, all-wise, all-good.

At the end of the day the most important thing is not how we pray — whether shouted or silent, scattered or centered, formal or spontaneous, speaking or listening. What matters most is that we pray, and the God we pray to.

12

COMPETENT TO SERVE

More than a half-century has passed since my ordination to Christian ministry. I had graduated from seminary, served two years as a student pastor, and completed the final interviews. I was declared competent to be a minister of the gospel. The ordination service was held in my home church on a Sunday morning, but I don't remember much about the ceremony. I do recall kneeling in front of the congregation while several older ministers laid hands on my head and prayed.

But there was a problem. Those elders didn't rest their hands politely on my head, leaving my hair unruffled. They pushed. They bore down. They tried to drive me into the floor – or was that just my perception? Whatever happened, the memory reminds me that serving the gospel is a weighty responsibility.

Competence doesn't necessarily depend on training or commissioning of any kind. George Lyman Kittredge taught English literature at Harvard from age 28 to 76. His Shakespearean scholarship was world-renowned, but he had no advanced degree. When asked why he never got a doctorate, he replied, "Who would examine me?" His competence was so clear that it was self-authenticating.

When I was in graduate school, a fellow student was specializing in the theology of Wolfhart Pannenberg. Eventually the time came for Frank to take the four-hour comprehensive exams in his field. According to the reports he began to write, but wadded up the paper and threw it down. He began again, only to crumple his work and throw it down. This continued for an hour until his nerves and his mind got together. Then he wrote furiously for the remaining time and passed with flying colors.

Later, when he submitted his dissertation on Pannenberg to a publisher, they laid aside other manuscripts in order to publish Frank's. Why? Because he had studied under the great German, and his competence came from that extended personal interaction.

For Christian workers, competence depends on more than churchly ordination or professional licensure. It comes from extended interaction with the living Lord. St. Paul struggled with this issue because he didn't know Jesus in the days of his flesh. Further, he had no letters of reference from the apostles who had walked with Christ.

Instead, he wrote, "our competence is from God, who has made us competent to be ministers of a new covenant, not of letter but of spirit; for the letter kills, but the Spirit gives life" (2 Cor. 3:5b-6). Where there is life-giving ministry in Jesus' name, where people are liberated through experience with the living Lord, where the Spirit empowers for faithful, obedient service, God-given competence is at work.

Britain's Eric Liddell entered the 1924 Olympics almost certain to win in the 100-meter dash, but he refused to compete. His reason? The preliminary heats were to be run on Sunday, and it was Liddell's conviction not to compete on the Lord's day. Britain's hopes for a gold medal were dashed. Then a few days later Liddell defeated two of the best competitors in the 400 meters, setting a new world record. "God made me fast," he said, "and when I run, I feel his pleasure." Human competence and divine joy – two sides of one coin.

Later, as a missionary in China (1925-43), Liddell was imprisoned when Japanese troops overran the country during World War II. His faithful witness and humble service inspired fellow internees. The guards even trusted him to cook for them, knowing he would not poison their food. Extended interaction with his Lord made him a beacon of light in the gray horror of the prison camp. His competence was one of character and, although he suffered from overwork and the brain tumor that killed him, he won The Race. Like the apostle, his competence to serve came from God. There is no higher source. There is no greater joy.

13

BLOW THE TRUMPET SOFTLY

The telephone call was abrupt. "J. D. died yesterday. The cancer came back with a rush. People were asked not to visit so that he and Jean could share their last days together in private."

So J. D. is dead. It doesn't seem possible. We've known it would come. He's been seriously ill for a long time. But now J. D. is gone, and with his going I experience a flood of memories that reach back to my high school years when I first met him. He gave me early opportunities in ministry by asking me to work with him. He gave me later opportunities by asking me to speak for special weeks in his church. I preached, he gave an evangelistic invitation, and God honored the work. We were as different as you can imagine, and I am grateful for his presence in my life. He wasn't perfect, but God used him in remarkable ways.

Fired by the flamethrowers of the South Pacific, J. D. rushed into ministry out of World War II. He hit the college campus running – some days running after his Jean and other days running from the terrors of his past.

He had led troops in ferocious combat. He saw his men, his friends, destroyed in the savagery that is war. He said the God he scarcely believed in had saved his life so he could save the lives of others. He was a brand from the burning, a red-hot ember intent on setting as many other fires as he could.

J. D. never met a stranger. When he left seminary for pastoral work, everyone nearby heard of him and, through him, of his Commanding Officer. Whether in a farming community or a metropolitan area, he was all over the map – pastor, radio evangelist, member of auxiliary organizations, consultant to the mayor, chaplain of the fire department, the one who talked would-be suicides down from tall buildings. He worked at ministry with a rush that was breathtaking. Babies, widows, homeowners, tough hombres, dropout kids – no one could hold out for long against his unstoppable love, his unquenchable energy, his indomitable spirit.

Ohio, Illinois, Indiana, Florida – wherever he went, counties heard, people smiled, churches grew, and lives were changed. The cross was his passion, the world was his parish. His love never seemed to suffer embarrassment or hesitation. He spoke frankly, boldly, courageously, tenderly, lovingly – always lovingly. He loved God and people and wanted only to bring them together in the Christ who had loved him from the South Pacific to South Bend.

But now J. D. is dead. Like the good soldier he was, he never quit, he never surrendered. The trumpet he used to play is stilled, and another will sound "Taps" at his grave. The pastor has closed his ministry. The trooper is laid to rest. The saint has gone to glory. Blow the trumpet softly. Play it slowly: "Amazing grace, how sweet the sound . . ."

14

A CAUSE FOR GIVING THANKS

Shortly after my wife and I moved to Pasadena, we drove the freeway for the first time. The Los Angeles freeway system was up and running, but nothing like it is today. We wanted to visit a cousin who lived south of us in Long Beach. She gave us clear directions which basically said, "Get on the freeway and stay in the left lane because you're coming all the way down." We did so, got off at the right exit, and had a joyful visit. On our return trip we repeated the process, but with a difference.

The Pasadena Freeway was, even then, one of the oldest in the L.A. system. It had numerous curves in it and trees growing in the median. Apparently it was designed for scenic value more than speed. As we rounded one of the curves northbound in the left lane, the Chevy died. It had brought us without incident from Ohio down Route 66 to southern California, but now it died.

I glanced at the dashboard and saw the temperature

gauge was as hot as it could get. A radiator hose, supposedly replaced, had burst and the engine had stalled. Jumping out, I ran to the car behind us. Above the screech of braking tires farther back I shouted, "Help me get off the road!" The driver didn't move. He only screamed out the window, "Get off the freeway!"

Within seconds a motorcycle police officer roared up. Instantly he blocked all northbound lanes of traffic. Then he did an amazing thing. He ordered the driver behind us to use his car to push ours across all the blocked lanes to a pull-off on the freeway's right side.

The rush of traffic resumed as the officer walked to my car window and asked, "What seems to be the trouble?" I told him what I could, and he radioed for a tow truck (this was b.c. – before cell phones or car phones). As he was leaving I asked, "How did you get here so quick?" "I was on the other side," he said, "and saw you were in trouble, so I came over."

We drove that freeway at other times and saw again the curve where we had broken down. A reinforced chain-link fence ran through the planted median strip as far as the eye could see. There were no crossovers, no openings in that fence.

What did the officer mean when he said, "I saw you . . . and I came over"? There was no place to cross – none. Did he fly over? Was he an angel? Can angels wear police uniforms and ride motorcycles?

To this day we have no explanation for what happened. But it reminds me of what God has done: "I saw you were in trouble, so I came over." That is God's action in the Word becoming flesh. That is God's action in the life and work of Jesus. That is God's action in our individual lives.

The message is "I am with you," and it is cause for giving thanks.

More recently, a group of travelers in the Arctic got lost when a sudden snowstorm blew in. They were away from the lodge where they were staying and became disoriented. The situation was more than dangerous – it was desperate. At last they were able to tramp back to the lodge and tell their story. As the group spokesman recounted what had happened, a listener remarked, "I guess your prayers were answered, weren't they?" The spokesman responded, "Hell, no! Some Eskimo came out of nowhere and showed us how to get back."

Now, if that's not an answer to prayer, what is? It echoes again God's action in Christ. The Word became flesh and made God known to us. He came out of "nowhere" and showed us how to get home. The message is "I am with you," and it is cause for giving thanks.

Hurricane Katrina ravaged our Gulf Coast states in 2005. It was the deadliest such storm in U.S. history. New Orleans became the symbol of all the cities damaged and drowned by the waters. In the aftermath thousands of people rushed in to help as they could. One of them was Steve, a young man from our church in Ohio. He worked for a time in Houston, Texas, with people who had fled the storm or had been transported out of New Orleans.

Eventually he needed to do laundry, so one evening he boarded a city bus with a pillowcase full of dirty clothes and the address of a laundromat on that route. He paid his fare, then asked the bus driver how many stops there would be to the laundromat. The driver said he didn't know of the place. Steve gave him the address, but the driver said there was no such address on his route.

So there he was, alone on a bus in the nation's fourth-largest city with his dirty clothes in a pillowcase, heading for a non-existent address. At that point, as Steve told the story, another passenger approached him. He appeared to be a homeless man. "I know where you're trying to go," he said. "There's a laundromat there." He gave Steve the name of the place and told him what bus stop to use. "And here," he added, "take my map of the bus routes. I don't need it anymore."

Once again God is at work: "I know where you're trying to go. . . . Take my map." The message is the same: "I am with you," and it is cause for giving thanks. Incidents such as these are God-sightings, thin places between us and the infinite. If we have eyes and hearts to recognize them, they call us again to give thanks, to express gratitude, to praise the One who said, "Remember, I am with you always, to the end of the age."

15

WHO AM I?

When my wife and I moved to Washington, D.C., we encountered traffic circles for the first time. We had been living in a village of one thousand in the Amish-Mennonite country of northern Indiana. It boasted a feed mill and a chicken processing plant, but no traffic lights. Julie taught music in two-room schools while I pastored a small congregation.

Moving to the nation's capital was a culture shock. Suddenly we encountered L'Enfant's traffic circles designed in 1791 for horses and carriages. The roundabouts could be frustrating, even terrifying. Three or four lanes of vehicles speed around Nascar-style with boulevards, avenues, and streets shooting off in all directions. Visitors have been known to circle for long periods of time, unable to decide where and how to exit. In biological terms, the circles are the city's ganglions, nerve junctions essential to its present life.

Human identity may be like that. I am a juncture where dynamic relationships revolve and intersect. As noted in the introduction to this book, I am simultaneously the son of my parents, the eldest of three brothers, the husband of one wife, the father of two daughters, and the grandfather of a couple young adults. My identity is where all of these meet, spin, and dance. That's the nucleus of who I am. That is my human identity, the core of my being. It's not a matter of job performance, achievement, or career. It's not about *doing* anything. I am a human *being* – and being is not merited or earned. It is received.

One of America's outstanding preachers, the late John Claypool, famously said that "life is gift – every last particle of it, and the way to handle a gift is to be grateful." He maintained that is true even when acute leukemia killed his daughter at the age of ten. Her life, he said, was a gift whether of ten days, ten months, or ten years.

Traffic circles often revolve around a statue, and sometimes a fountain. They may take their name from the person depicted in the center. As a follower of Jesus Christ, my most basic relationship is the one I have with him. It transcends and transfigures all other relationships. The core identity of all my intersecting circles is who I am in Christ. He's the center around which all else revolves, the fountain from which all life proceeds. That is pure grace, God's gift, deserving my gratitude.

No one understood it better than the young man from Tarsus who was unhorsed long ago outside Damascus. Blinded at first by his vision of the risen Lord, he later came to see life differently. One of the most significant expressions in the letters he wrote is the phrase "in Christ." Together with its variants, he said it about two hundred times. It must be important.

It's not a matter of "Jesus and me." This identity is indeed personal but not private, corporate as well as individual. It is life in the Body of which Christ is the Head. And, in Paul's terms, the head is the life-source. I am who I am in Christ. I am one branch of the vine that he is. I am in him together with you, all of us dependent on this One who is alive with the life of eternity.

In Christ the unknown god of Athens has become personally, permanently accessible. In Jesus we meet the invisible Yahweh of Israel in the flesh. His own Spirit, present, powerful, holy, resides in us and gifts us with our true identity. Children of the heavenly Father, joint heirs with Christ the Son, vessels of the Holy Spirit, intersections of this age and the age to come, ganglions of eternal life – our core identity is not static. Pulsating with life, it is God's dynamic gift to us. And the way to handle any gift is to be grateful. Amen?

16

PRACTICING THE PRESENCE: BROTHER LAWRENCE

During my thirties I was a busy pastor in Washington, D.C., in the middle of the civil rights movement and the cultural revolution of the sixties. At that time I bought my first copy of *The Practice of the Presence of God* – sixty-four pages for fifty cents. It is the second of the three devotional books I have read the most. Similar in some ways to Thomas Kelly, its author was quite opposite in others. Both were ambitious men, driven to follow what they perceived as God's call on their life. But there the similarities end.

Nicolas Herman was born in 1611 or 1614 in Lorraine, an area between France and Germany which belonged at that time to France. Unlike Germany, France had remained Catholic when the Protestant Reformation occurred. Nicolas grew up in a pious Catholic home, received rudimentary schooling, and as a teenager went off to the army. What history calls the Thirty Years' War had begun in 1618 and would drag on until 1648. The issue was whether the land should be

Catholic or some variety of Protestant, and the struggle was savage. Civilian populations suffered terribly as year after year armies rampaged back and forth destroying towns, burning crops, and brutalizing the populace.

Nicolas served in the French army and was captured by the Germans. They thought he was a spy and threatened to hang him, but his simple manner convinced them he was harmless. They sent him back to his own army. Apparently he wasn't even worth hanging. Later, in a battle against Swedish troops, he received a serious leg injury and was allowed to return home to recuperate. But the recovery was incomplete, forcing him to walk all his life with a pronounced limp.

When he was eighteen (before or during his military service – no one knows), he experienced a religious conversion. As he reported it, he noticed a tree bare in midwinter. He knew the tree would come to life in the spring, so he applied the idea to himself. Believing God loved him as well as the tree, Nicolas opened his heart, asking God to give him new life like the tree. It was as simple, as undramatic as that.

When he could no longer engage in military service, he changed careers. He became a servant in the household of a nobleman who was the king's treasurer. The king of France at the time was Louis XIV, the Sun King, builder of the famed palace at Versailles. But Nicolas was clumsy by nature, which his injured leg only made worse, and he kept breaking his employer's valuable possessions. So he was fired, another unwelcome change. His time in military and domestic service amounted to about eighteen years.

Now, wanting to give his life wholly to God, he tried a different kind of career. He attempted to live as a hermit, but that didn't work for him either. Finally a family member suggested that he try getting into a monastery. There he could live out his devotion to God in a community of like-minded men where he would find support and accountability. This would be his vocation for the rest of his life.

In 1642 Nicolas was admitted to a large monastery of the Discalced Carmelites in Paris. The monks spent much time in prayer and meditation along the lines set out by their founders, Teresa of Avila and John of the Cross. Nicolas proceeded through the stages of probation until he became an accepted lay brother with the name Lawrence of the Resurrection. He never advanced to the priesthood, however, but always remained just Brother Lawrence, one among the lowest group in the community. Founded in 1611, part of that extensive monastery has survived four hundred years and is still there today.

At first Brother Lawrence found the structured prayers and confessions to be difficult, for his spirit craved a more natural, spontaneous approach to God. Later he made no secret of how hard that time was. But he persevered in following the monastic rule for ten years, and then he had a breakthrough. Throwing himself on God's mercy, he told the Father that he would love him even if he were sent to hell. From then on, Brother Lawrence experienced an inner peace beyond anything he could describe.

He also realized that beyond the hours set for designated prayers he could pray as he wished. So on his own time he began to carry on a silent conversation with God, speaking personally and openly. He was a simple man, and he talked to God simply and frankly. He called it "the practice of the presence of God." He tried to think of God in each moment and fulfill his duties not merely out of obedience to his superiors, but from love for God.

Lay brothers were expected to pray and do manual

labor. Brother Lawrence's assignment was kitchen duty. He was a cook for the monastery, trying in its busy kitchen to do each thing in sequence for the love of God. With sometimes more than one hundred men to feed, this was no easy task. Occasionally the monastery sent him a long distance by riverboat to restock their wine supply. This made him nervous because he was not confident of handling the transactions well, and his leg bothered him a lot. It was so bad that on deck he could move around best by rolling himself from one barrel to another. But he accepted the assignment as from God, asking assistance to complete it, and at the end thanked God gratefully. He spent fifteen years in kitchen duty with its various responsibilities.

Word began to get out that there was a special man in the monastery, a man close to God, a holy man. It wasn't the abbot in charge or his assistant, the prior – it was the cook, plain Brother Lawrence. Monks and nuns in other places began writing to him, and an important priest interviewed him several times in 1666-67. Outwardly the former soldier seemed rather crusty and brusque, but the priest soon recognized the cook's genuine, tender heart. Meanwhile, as his leg continued to deteriorate, he was relieved of kitchen duty and assigned to the cobbler's shop. There he could sit while working to create or repair the sandals which the monks wore. Eventually his leg became diseased and ulcerated. Brother Lawrence suffered greatly and bravely until his spirit slipped away on February 12, 1691.

Following his death those who loved him began to exchange the letters he had written to them. The next year the priest who interviewed him published his notes from their four conversations together with sixteen letters from the last decade of the monk's life. But it was not a good time for that.

French Catholic leaders were embroiled in a controversy over "quietism" (a totally passive approach to prayer), and some of them thought what Brother Lawrence said sounded like that. So although many appreciated his simple, direct teaching based on the love of God, it was swept away and forgotten.

In England, however, people began to notice his approach as they read it in the original French. Then in 1724 *The Practice of the Presence of God* appeared in an English translation. From that time until now multitudes have read and honored Brother Lawrence as the author of a devotional classic. Nun Gabriela, sometimes called the Mother Teresa of Orthodox Christianity, said she held him in high regard. Among Protestants, Hannah Whitall Smith wrote one of the 19th century's most popular devotional books, *The Christian's Secret of a Happy Life*. She called Brother Lawrence's work "one of the most helpful books I know.... It fits into the lives of all human beings." Dean William Sperry of Harvard wrote, "What captivates us about the man is his candor, and his utter lack of anything approaching sentimentality. . . . Much of the difficulty which religion meets in its address to the world derives from a lack of precisely such blunt sincerity." Hal Helms, who edited a recent translation of *The Practice of the Presence of God*, said of Brother Lawrence, "We understand him and love him for his realistic honesty."

Realism, bluntness, candor, honesty — such down-to-earth traits have endeared the simple monk to thousands of readers. Even the brevity of his wisdom is attractive. *The Practice of the Presence of God* can be printed in a booklet slim enough to fit shirt-pocket or purse with scarcely a bulge.

Although never honored by his church, Brother Lawrence continues to bless readers today. His sense of God's care and closeness is inviting. His love for God and his message to keep our love simple remain gifts to the church. His stress on persistent moment-by-moment prayerfulness sounds like Thomas Kelly's wisdom. But the two men could not be more different. Dr. Kelly was a Quaker, a family man, highly educated, and widely traveled. Brother Lawrence was a Catholic, a monk, a man of little schooling who traveled only when ordered to do so.

The most famous passage in his writing may be this one: "The times of activity are not at all different from the hours of prayer," he said, "for I possess God as peacefully in the commotion of my kitchen, where often enough several people are asking me for different things at the same time, as I do when kneeling before the Blessed Sacrament. . . . I flip my little omelette in the frying pan for the love of God, and when . . . I can do nothing else, it is enough for me to pick up a straw from the ground for the love of God."

Who would not want such stability, such centeredness, or – in Thomas Kelly's terms – such integration of life?

17

THE WORLD MY PARISH

During seven years of pastoral work in Washington, D.C., I presided at several burials in Arlington National Cemetery. Established during the Civil War, its 624 acres today contain 400,000 graves of American military personnel and specified family members. To walk and work, however briefly, in that great city of the dead is a moving experience.

The committal service never fails to be impressive. When the pastor is finished, the honor guard with seemingly no command lifts the American flag that has covered the casket. In reverent silence their gloved hands fold it into a neat, tight triangle. Then it is presented to the next of kin, a token of thanks from a grateful nation. A bugler sounds "Taps," and the ceremony is over. Pride and gratitude mingle with grief and loss, and tears are always present.

President Calvin Coolidge once said, "We want peace and honor, and that charity which is so strong an element of all civilization. The chief ideal of the American people is idealism. America is a nation of idealists." I am profoundly thankful to be a citizen of the land of the free, the home of the brave. And I want to use that privilege for the good of others.

In ancient Israel, Samuel served as prophet, priest, and judge. When his nation decided they wanted a king like their neighbors, he believed they were rejecting God's leadership. He anointed tall, handsome Saul as Israel's first monarch, then offered this comment: "Moreover, as for me, far be it from me that I should sin against the Lord by ceasing to pray for you" (1 Sam. 12:23).

How can prophets, how can anyone best pray for their nation? Karl Barth famously said we should do it with the Bible in one hand and the day's newspaper in the other. Current events are not just news, they are a call to prayer. In today's world, what happens anywhere can be momentarily in our hand, before our eyes, and in our face.

John Wesley chose not to confine his interest to the borders tradition placed around him. "The world is my parish," he said. And with prayer and persistence he spent himself for that world.

One songwriter in ancient Israel felt the same way.

> *May God be gracious to us and bless us*
> *and make his face to shine upon us,*
> *that your way may be known upon earth,*
> *your saving power among all nations.*
> *Let the peoples praise you, O God;*
> *let all the peoples praise you.* . . .
> *May God continue to bless us;*
> *let all the ends of the earth revere him.*
> (Ps. 67:1-3, 7)

For that poet, Israel was to be God's leaven in the

world, God's salt and light for the nations.

Today, more than ever, God's people are called to pray "for kings and all who are in high positions, so that we may lead a quiet and peaceable life in all godliness and dignity." Beyond our desire for peace and quiet lies the will of the God "who desires everyone to be saved and to come to the knowledge of the truth" (1 Tim. 2:2, 4).

For that purpose we might pray as A. B. Simpson, founder of the Christian and Missionary Alliance, prayed – with arms wrapped around a globe. Or we might open ourselves to pray with World Vision's founder Bob Pierce, "Let my heart be broken with the things that break the heart of God." And, imperfect as he was, Pierce spent himself for the sake of the world.

In 1727, John Ward, Member of Parliament for Melcome and Regis, wrote a prayer that has become sadly famous. "O Lord, you know that I have nine houses in the city of London, and that I have recently purchased an estate in Essex. Please keep the two counties of Middlesex [the site of London] and Essex from fires and earthquakes. And, as I have also a mortgage in Hertfordshire, I beg you also to have an eye of compassion on that county, and the rest of the counties you may treat as you like. . . ."

God, bless America – "and the rest of the [nations] you may treat as you like"? Not if the world is my parish. Not if God wants all people to be saved. Not if I open my heart to brokenness on behalf of the globe.

President Coolidge was right: America is a nation of idealists. God forbid that we should sin by forgetting our ideals or failing to pray for this nation. Then we can spend ourselves for the sake of the world.

18

A COST TO CONSIDER,
A RISK TO TAKE

"Mr. Flora, we have a problem." My doctoral supervisor was speaking. We had gone to lunch and now were sitting in the front seat of his Volkswagen Beetle. All the way through Louisville city traffic and all during lunch he had talked about the car. He related how he bought it in Germany while on sabbatical leave and had it shipped to Kentucky. He rhapsodized about what kind of mileage it got and how much he enjoyed driving it.

Now we were back on campus, and I was about to open the door. "Mr. Flora, we have a problem. You have been in the doctoral program for some time now. In the seminars and colloquia you remain silent. Some of the students feel that you have answers and insights, but you refuse to share them."

I had experienced "a call to the ministry" at thirteen. After college and seminary I completed an advanced master's degree, then became a full-time pastor. Ten years and two churches later I felt I was called to graduate-level teaching. That would require a doctorate. Now I was head to head with students who were a decade younger than I – and I was a decade behind.

"Mr. Flora, there is no life without pain. But sometimes you may choose your pain. In this situation you may choose to remain silent, and risk being misunderstood. Or you may speak up, and risk being wrong. So choose your pain." In the Beetle's front seat there was no place to hide. I knew he was right. Here was a cost to the call this introvert had not considered.

There are varieties of call and varieties of cost, but there is always risk. We are challenged to step out of our comfort zone, confront the unknown, and walk on what seems like water. There are no guarantees of success. Prophets cannot count on being honored. In fact, in some ancient Jewish thinking, the call to be a prophet implied a destiny of martyrdom. There were traditions that said both Isaiah and Jeremiah died because they obeyed their calls.

The very process of growing up involves painful experience. Famed Washington, D.C. pastor Gordon Cosby used to say, "No one reaches adulthood unwounded." Beyond that the call to discipleship involves risk, for God doesn't show the end from the beginning. "Follow me" – those are almost the first and last words Jesus spoke to Simon Peter who, early tradition says, paid for his faith with his life. Similarly, one account of Paul's conversion says, "I myself will show him how much he must suffer for the sake of my name" (Acts 9:16). Working under the nose of the Nazis, Dietrich Bonhoeffer wrote, "When Christ calls a man, he bids him come and die." A few years later he became one of the last century's most famous Christian martyrs.

The call to Christian service usually entails a call to prepare. Counselors, entrepreneurs, pastors, local church workers – all must prepare. That may mean study or apprenticeship or travel. It will definitely demand time, effort, and discipline. To illustrate the costly discipline – the "suffering" – in obeying the call, St. Paul likened it to military service, athletic competition, and labor-intensive farming (2 Tim. 2).

Whether in basic training or active deployment, in call or service, there is always a cost to consider and a risk to take. When the eternal Son fell into the virgin's womb, as Julian of Norwich put it, there was unfathomable cost and risk. When the lion of Judah became the lamb who takes away the sin of the world, the same was true. And when you or I answer our call with "Here am I, use me," we fulfill Oswald Chambers' words. We become broken bread and poured-out wine for the sake of the world. But we must not complain about the fingers God uses to squeeze us with.

Or, as another has said, "God does not call the qualified, but qualifies the called." And for all who respond there will be a cost to consider, a risk to take. The front seat of a Beetle is a good place to learn that.

19

MICKEY'S LEGACY

I want to tell you – I must tell you – about Michael, or Mickey as I learned to call him. The first time I saw him he was firmly planted in his wheelchair. I had come to a weekend retreat, and there he sat across the meeting room. He looked intriguing, even intimidating, dressed as he was completely in black. His clothing from head to foot was all black – shirt and trousers, socks and shoes. On his head sat a black seaman's watchcap below which sprouted a short black beard. On his hands he wore black leather gloves with the fingertips cut out. All told, he was a dark, heavy, imposing figure.

At mealtime we had to go up two half-flights of steps to reach the dining room. I fell in line near him, and we prepared to ascend together. But it was no easy task. His folded wheelchair became my responsibility. The steps were his Mount Everest. Slowly, with enormous effort he hauled himself up with the help of the handrail. If the rail had not been sturdily anchored into the wall, he could not have climbed the steps. After what seemed like an eternity in slow motion we arrived at the table.

I sat across from him as he introduced himself. "I'm Michael," he growled. A gap or two was visible in his teeth. "I'm an ol' Kentucky bear." With that he began to talk about his love for his home state, especially its eastern hills, where he had lived in his early years. He was an interesting conversationalist, but I could not guess his age because his black beard showed no gray in it.

Michael belonged to a small, informal community of men who considered themselves followers of St. Francis of Assisi. They lived simply in order to serve urban street people. His all-black garb was a private testimony to this semi-monastic commitment. He spoke about Chicago and Atlanta, where his community worked with the homeless. But now due to deteriorating health he was in Ohio with family nearby.

As our weekend retreat moved toward its conclusion, we had an evening prayer service that concluded with holy communion. Our group gathered in the small stone chapel of the retreat center. The service was like many before it with lights lowered and prayers murmured softly. At its close people were free to leave as they wished, but a friend and I chose to linger. For over at the side, next to a large stone pillar, sat Michael in his wheelchair. He was different now, somehow agitated. He was rocking forward and back, forward and back, his lips moving silently, his face contorted.

Sensing that something important was happening, my friend and I moved over to him. Without speaking we stood alongside, placing our hands on his black-capped head. In the silence we prayed intensely and wordlessly for this broken hulk of a man, his body so much beyond his control but his mind as good as ever. Then after long minutes we left, silently.

Michael later wrote to me about the experience, the first of a couple dozen letters that passed between us before he died. He explained that after we prayed that night, the tears had come. Tears he had dammed up for years. Tears of a grief so deep his broken body could not express it. Tears of a broken heart for Heather, his beloved fiancée, who died shortly before their wedding. For twelve years he had soldiered on alone, but at last he was able to shed the tears of grief which might become healing tears for him.

We began an occasional correspondence, only now he insisted that I call him Mickey. Others might call him Michael, but as he put it, "I don't cotton to Mike." He made it clear that only a select few were invited to call him Mickey, but he never explained the reason for his preference. Although his physical limitations confined him to his wheelchair and his apartment, he had a ministry of prayer and encouragement for others. His handwriting was almost indecipherable, so he would crank notepaper or a greeting card into his old typewriter and then type onto it. Messages from him were almost always written in capital letters. It suited him to put on the shift lock and bang away in large type, often ignoring any kind of punctuation.

Gradually I learned that his troubles began when he was very small. According to his account, at the age of two he was thrown through the window of a house, landing outside on concrete. The fall caused brain damage, loss of vision in one eye, and impaired hearing. Special education classes got him through public school, after which he trained to be a licensed practical nurse. Six years before I met him he had suffered a stroke which caused him to fall down two outdoor flights of steps and left him wheelchair bound. The stroke and fall produced additional damage in the same area of his brain. He experienced intense pain there which was now found to be caused by a tumor in an advanced state. Because he had serious heart problems, surgery was out of the question. The man was dying, and it was in that condition I first met him.

Although Mickey was an ordained Protestant minister, he felt drawn to aspects of the Catholic Church. Not only was he in the tradition of St. Francis, he also enjoyed visits to the Trappist monastery in Kentucky where Thomas Merton had lived. Holy ground, he called it. There he renewed his love for monastic life and his native bluegrass state.

But clearly, the best thing that ever happened to him was Heather, the love of his life, and losing her left him with aching grief. As our correspondence deepened he often spoke of her, and of God as Daddy. Death was a friend he expected to meet in the near future. He did not fear it – he welcomed it. Death would mean sloughing off his broken body. It would mean release from constant pain, reunion with his beloved Heather, and being at home with Daddy.

Although he could write seriously of these matters, Mickey was not morbid. Humor peeked between the lines of his all-capital communiqués, and a gritty faith showed through as well. If good humor is a trait of maturity, then Mickey possessed a mature spirit. His faith shone warmly as he often encouraged me or composed a prayer for me. His written prayers usually took the form of a benediction, such as this one:

MAY THE LORD BLESS YOU AND KEEP YOU
MAY HE POUR DOWN OVER YOU HIS HOLY FIRE
MAY YOUR HEART BE SET TO HOLY DANCE
AND MAY YOUR VOICE BE FILLED
WITH THE SOUNDS OF HIS ANGELS

Or this one, like the first, unpunctuated and in capital letters:

MAY THE LORD BLESS YOU AND KEEP YOU
MAY HE KEEP YOUR VOICE AND FEET STRONG
AS YOU TEACH
MAY HE ALSO BRING YOU OFTEN TO SILENCE
AND THROUGH THIS SILENCE MAY YOU ALWAYS
HAVE THE GIFT OF LISTENING

Mickey's health steadily declined, and he needed constant assistance with his living. The tumor continued its relentless advance until at last he got his wish. Sister Death called for him and carried him to meet Heather and the Daddy they both loved so much.

Why am I telling you all this? First, because Mickey reminds me even now that a broken body and a burdened spirit can still carry the light of Christ. My friend was a man of deep pain and great faith, but he was not healed until death. No matter how many prayers were spoken, he – like Elisha and Trophimus and St. Paul – had to contend with illness and suffering. Still he persevered. Still he trusted. Still he encouraged others until relieved of his post.

I'm also telling you this because he closed most of his correspondence using the same words: "PEACE. JOY. WONDER." I asked myself, how could a man in his condition choose such words to bless others? I came to believe it was because Mickey knew he was not the center of his own life. He did not demand to be in control, in charge, on top.

Instead, like St. Francis, who was blind and broken in body before he died at age forty-five, Mickey worshiped. In his final year Francis composed the prayer we know as "The Canticle of the Sun." There he praised God for Brother Sun and Sister Moon, for Brother Fire and Sister Water, for wind and air, fruits and flowers, and even for Sister Death. For Mickey, scripture and recorded music, corporate worship and spiritual retreats, extensive reading, and correspondence with friends all became avenues of nurture for himself and service to others. That's why he could sign off with "PEACE. JOY. WONDER."

A famous tyrant once defined peace as the period after one war when a nation prepares for the next. Tragically, human history has been written in just those terms. But biblically, peace is more than the absence of conflict. It is positive, not negative. It is *shalom*, the presence of everything that makes life worthwhile. It involves body and soul, flesh and spirit, others and earth, self and God. It includes the created world we call nature and all that sustains us in it. "Peace" was both hello and goodbye for ancient Hebrews, and St. Paul wrote it at the beginning and end of all his letters. It was the word Jesus used to bless his disciples before his arrest, and it was the way he greeted them after his resurrection.

Joy is more than happiness. Happiness depends on circumstances. Joy depends on character. Happiness comes from externals. Joy bubbles up from inside. Happiness may arise from things. Joy includes people. Joy comes from being appreciated and validated and loved. Ultimately, joy arises from relationship with the living God whose infinite, eternal love spills over in the creation of the universe and the liberation of its wayward citizens.

Wonder is the open spirit of small children discovering the world for themselves. Every day is a new adventure with sunrise and soap bubbles and butterflies and spider webs and silly songs and funny flavors. St. Francis did not let misunderstanding, opposition, or ill health keep him from seeing the wonder of Brother Sun, "who brings the day," and Sister Moon, "bright and precious and fair." Or Sister Earth, "who feeds us in her sovereignty and produces various fruits with colored flowers and herbs." The ultimate wonder is that the God of the universe has stooped in Christ to become one of us so we may have life, and have it to the full. We may not know what the future holds, but we trust we shall be like him, for we shall see him as he is.

C. S. Lewis was right. This world is like a sculptor's shop filled with partially finished statues. They – we – stand, sit, or lie in various positions and in varying stages of development. But there's a rumor going around the shop that one of these days all the statues are going to come to life – Mickey and Heather, you and I, all of us. And on that day there will be PEACE. JOY. WONDER. WITHOUT END.

Such is Mickey's legacy.

20

A VOICE OF LOVE

Twice in my life I have been in counseling. In both periods of counseling I noted how good it felt to have an appointment. Just to know that in so-many days ahead I could unload on an "outsider" gave me hope. It helped to keep me going. Of course, the outsiders were competent professionals, not close friends. On health matters friends may share personal experience or perhaps medical advice, but there comes a time when we need trained nurses, doctors, and specialists.

The counselors didn't solve my problems or fix me. Instead, they offered understanding and insight, voiced suggestions and encouragement. Although I left each session feeling lighter, I knew I still had to exercise faith and fortitude, and follow through on what they said.

I wonder about other believers I've heard of. Would they have been better off with counseling? Would it have brought Augustine to a more healthy sense of human sexuality, or resolved the contradictory elements in Martin Luther's personality? Would counseling have made John Wesley's marriage as happy as his brother Charles's, or lifted Charles

Spurgeon's depression to make him a better preacher?

One instance where it did help is close at hand. The late Henri Nouwen needed and received in-depth counseling at a painful time of his life. As a Catholic priest he was carefully trained in theology, then spent a decade in advanced studies in psychology. He taught at Notre Dame University, then at Yale and Harvard divinity schools, but resigned from all three. Priest yes, professor no. At heart he was a pastor, a shepherd of souls.

Sensing this, Toronto's L'Arche community invited Henri Nouwen to join them. L'Arche communities are group homes for people with mental disabilities, but distinctive because "clients" and their caretakers live together. So Nouwen became the live-in pastor for his community. Although he was happier than at any time in his life, he was still the same sensitive, needy person he'd always been. When an especially close friend pulled away because of that, the pastor spiraled down into clinical depression.

For seven months in another city he received intensive care from highly skilled therapists and spiritual directors. With their help he began to improve and experience healing. Each day he wrote a few lines of encouragement for himself in a secret journal. It helped him keep his head above the depression that threatened to drown him.

Back in Toronto, Nouwen hesitantly allowed a few friends to see what he had written. Unanimous that this material was so human, so godly, and so wise, they persuaded him to publish it. *The Inner Voice of Love: A Journey Through Anguish to Freedom* went on sale the day a heart attack took its author's life in 1996. Some reviewers consider it the most focused, most powerful of all his forty books.

His journey through anguish to freedom reminds me

that all of us, despite our dysfunctions, are valuable. Skilled professionals can help us to offer not just what we do, but who we are for the glory of God and our neighbor's good.

As Nouwen wrote in his book's closing words, "I have heard the inner voice of love, deeper and stronger than ever. I want to keep trusting in that voice and be led by it beyond the boundaries of my short life, to where God is all in all." Thanks to good counselors, I can say that too.

21

REVEALING DIVINE LOVE: JULIAN OF NORWICH

People who enjoy a good mystery may also like Julian of Norwich. This woman of prayer lived for decades in a tiny apartment or cell attached to the church of St. Julian in Norwich, England. She is called by the name of that church, but who she was or how she got there or what became of her, no one knows. At her death she left behind the first book written in English by a woman.

Thomas Merton, whose learning was encyclopedic, valued her as one of the two greatest English theologians – far better, he said, than all the Spanish mystics taken together. We know her today as both a uniquely creative theologian and a devotional writer of extraordinary optimism and grace. She is the third of my longest-standing devotional favorites, encountered first in my fifties.

Julian was born in 1342 and lived through one of the most horrific periods in England's history. When she was seven years old the bubonic plague, after sweeping through

Europe, jumped the English Channel and killed one-third of her country's population. Some estimates put the death toll as high as one-half. No one understood its cause or cure. Conventional wisdom held it to be the terrifying judgment of God. A dozen years later it returned, this time especially striking down young children. It appeared in Norwich for the third time in 1368, when Julian was twenty-six. The disease – variously called the black death for the way it darkened the skin or bubonic plague for its trademark buboes (swellings) – killed its victims in a matter of days, sometimes within hours.

As if this were not enough, the 14th century in general was one of the hardest in English history. There was prolonged war because the king of England was claiming to be also the king of France. Internal unrest turned violent in 1381 when peasants revolted against the monarchy. At the same time Oxford University professor John Wycliffe began translating the New Testament from the church's Latin into the language of the people. The university, considered the spiritual center of England, expelled him when he attacked the papacy as Antichrist. In the years that followed some who adopted his ideas were burned at the stake less than two miles from the church of St. Julian.

No one knows just when the woman we call Julian came to live at the church, but her action was not unusual for the time. She was an anchoress, a professional intercessor and spiritual director in residence. A man or woman who lived this way was often called a recluse, and prosperous Norwich claimed dozens of them. The vocation was popular enough that manuals were developed for its conduct and practice.

If Julian's situation followed the manuals, she would be permanently enclosed in one or two small rooms attached to the church. A walled garden area might be just outside.

Her apartment or cell would have a squint, a narrow window into the church through which she could observe the daily hours of prayer and receive the bread of the eucharist (only priests received the wine). Another window would face the street, in her case the busy road southwest toward London. If she was available for conversation, the window would be open but covered with a white cloth to hide her face. And we know that Julian was available because Margery Kempe, famed for her travel to holy sites, recorded that she visited Julian, who encouraged her with good advice.

The manuals for anchoresses allowed them to have a servant to bring in provisions and run necessary errands. They also could have a cat for companionship and rodent control. Their task was to anchor the church by praying. They were to pray with the church in its daily hours of worship and pray for the church in every conceivable way. Everything was grist for prayer – births, baptisms, confirmations, marriages, deaths, planting, harvesting, herds, flocks, king and country, bishop and priest, city and parish. Anything could be subject for prayer together with the cultivation of one's own soul.

No one knows how long Julian lived this kind of life or when she died. In her later years she received money from several bequests, the last in 1416 when she would have been in her mid-seventies. She died sometime after that, but when or where she was laid to rest remains a mystery. She simply disappeared from history.

By the time her life ended the Italian Renaissance was in full bloom, Robin Hood had appeared in popular English literature, Geoffrey Chaucer had written his *Canterbury Tales*, Joan of Arc was born (1412), and Professor Jan Hus had been burned at the stake for promoting Wycliffe's ideas at the University of Prague (1415). Within a century a German professor named Luther would light the fires of the Reformation, changing forever the history and character of Europe.

An early scribe who copied Julian's book called it *Revelations of Divine Love* because that's what the book is about. Julian preferred to call her experiences simply *Showings*. She expounds a series of visions and words from the Lord which she received at the age of thirty in May 1373. She had prayed to identify so closely with Christ's sufferings that she could feel what he felt. She became gravely ill, and a parish priest administered the church's last rites. When he left Julian, he placed a crucifix before her and encouraged her to take comfort from the Lord who suffered on the cross for her. As she tried to focus on the crucifix she said Christ began to speak to her. Sixteen "showings" followed in the next twenty-four hours, after which they stopped and she fully recovered. It never happened again. She wrote down what she experienced and what she thought it meant. Then she kept quiet. For nearly twenty years she thought and prayed, then wrote a longer version of what happened and what it meant. The book exists today in both the early short text and the more definitive longer version.

The basic message is that God's love is so all-encompassing it meets every need and satisfies every longing. She concludes that in all God showed her and told her "love was his meaning." If that is true, then "all shall be well, and all shall be well, and all manner of things shall be well." These statements – maybe her most memorable ones – come at the end of the book, which describes her sixteen "showings" in eighty-six chapters.

She begins by relating her dying experience and the vision she had of the dying Christ. Her description of his body hanging in a dry, icy wind is especially striking. But more important to Julian is that Jesus did this out of love for her and all believers – and if he could do more, he would. True love produces both sacrifice and joy, and he speaks to her of both. Although a handful of early chapters contain graphic descriptions of his suffering, Julian writes mostly about the love of God in Christ, from which nothing can separate us.

One of the book's most famous passages is the hazelnut vision of chapter 5, which contains echoes of Augustine's *Confessions*. It speaks of our restlessness apart from the God who made us for himself. The mystery of Julian deepens because no one knows if she had read Augustine, assuming she could read, or if she merely heard his kind of language where she was. Of course, behind both the African orator and the English visionary lie the words of Jesus "Come to me, all you that are weary and are carrying heavy burdens, and I will give you rest. Take my yoke upon you, and learn from me; for I am gentle and humble in heart, and you will find rest for your souls" (Matt. 11:28-29).

Julian loves to employ threefold statements in her writing. Even more, she is thoroughly trinitarian in her thinking and Christ-centered in focus. As she says, "Where Jesus is spoken of, the Holy Trinity is to be understood" (chap. 4). She takes three chief attributes of God and identifies them with the members of the godhead: the power or might of the Father, the wisdom of the Son, and the Spirit's goodness or love. Whenever I sing "Awesome God," Rich Mullins' popular praise song, I am reminded of Julian's understanding of the wisdom, power and love of the three-personed God. For Julian, God as Father, Son, and Holy Spirit is all mighty, all wise, and all good.

Present-day writers call Jesus Lord, as Julian does, but

she also refers to the Holy Spirit as Lord. In doing so she echoes the ancient Nicene and Athanasian creeds which speak of "the Lord the Spirit." Following biblical precedent, she flexes between God as God and the Father as God. But when it comes to the Son, Julian explodes in creativity. She employs a whole volley of terms for who Christ Jesus is – brother, savior, spouse, friend, lord – he is, in fact, our heaven (chap. 19).

Julian has received much attention in our day because she also calls Jesus our mother. She sees in him the tenderness and nurturing which people often identify with motherhood. But there is more. Julian also sees in Jesus the wisdom of God – profound compassionate, truthful understanding and guidance. When the Bible was read in her church, always in Latin, the term "wisdom" was feminine. In ancient Hebrew and Greek, as well as Latin, wisdom is a feminine term. Even today many people associate wisdom with a grandmother or another woman rich in experience – a spiritual mother. For Julian, Jesus is the mother whose pain on the cross gave birth to the church and who continues to nourish his people through word and sacrament. But Julian does not replace God the Father with God the Mother. Instead, she cracks the rules of grammar when she writes, "Jesus our mother, he does...," or "he says..."

However motherly Jesus is, for Julian he is always Lord. She sees him as a joyful monarch, ranging through a great banquet hall to greet his guests and make them at home in his home (chap. 14). Jesus is, in fact, both "courteous" and "homely." He has all the dignity and manners of the royal court. At the same time he enjoys being at home with the least of his subjects. This king would enjoy coffee at the kitchen table.

No one is too small or unnoticed for his attention — and that care is all wise, all mighty, and all loving. Our experience alternates between weal and woe. Our lives swing like pendulums between despair and joy. But Jesus' desire is always for our comfort in both solace and strength. Julian notes that what she saw and heard is for all Christians, for Christ wants us to rest in him, love him, and enjoy him forever.

Sin and its effects are what bother us, and Julian too. If God is love, as she says, then why do we suffer? Even more, why does God allow sin in the world? Julian received no answer to this in her revelations. It remained for her, as for us, life's great unresolved tension. What she did hear was a word from God. At the last day there will be "a great deed" in which God will make all things right. Only God knows the details of that deed or its date, and we are not to speculate about it. "I saw our Lord's purpose quite clearly: the more anxious we are to discover his secret knowledge about this or anything else, the further we shall be from knowing it" (chap. 33). Instead, we are to remember what God has already done, learn from that, and so rest in him. We are to persevere in believing, trusting, and risking all in love.

With that sunny faith, that serious optimism, Julian asserts what she learned in her showings: "All shall be well, and all shall be well, and all manner of things shall be well." This is no mindless self-hypnosis. It grows, rather, out of her immersion in scripture. She would have heard the Psalms in her church every day throughout her years as an anchoress. In addition, her writing gives evidence of being especially formed by the Fourth Gospel and the letters of Paul. Her general tone echoes the triumphant conclusion of Romans 8 that nothing can separate us from the love of God which is in

Christ Jesus our Lord.

Showings seems almost to be an extended meditation on ideas and language such as that — and this: "God is love, and those who abide in love abide in God, and God abides in them. . . . There is no fear in love, but perfect love casts out fear . . . We love because he first loved us" (1 John 4:16b, 18-19).

Julian's book is long and sometimes repetitious. Excellent abridged versions and selections have been produced by such writers as Sheila Upjohn and Keith Beasley-Topliffe. Ms. Upjohn lives near Julian's church in Norwich and has studied her writing for most of her life. I'm a relative newcomer, but after twenty-five years her book still encourages me. In the words of the blind Scottish pastor-poet George Matheson, she writes of a "love that will not let me go." And so "I rest my weary soul" and "give back the life I owe."

22

WATCH OUT FOR MOTORCYCLES!

Not far from where I live there are dangerous highway intersections. One in particular has proved deadly through the years. It's where a two-lane highway crosses US 30, a four-lane divided national highway.

An especially tragic accident occurred there a while back. A guy and his girlfriend were cruising along the divided highway on his motorcycle. A driver in a pickup truck pulled out in front of them without seeing them. The bike rider swerved to avoid hitting the pickup but could not miss it entirely. He clipped the truck's rear corner, which caused him to lose control of the motorcycle. He and his girlfriend were both ejected, but neither was wearing a helmet. She died instantly, and the emergency squad found him in critical condition. A helicopter life-flighted him to an urban trauma center, and that's where the newspaper story ended.

The tragedy reminded me of yard signs and bumper stickers that say, "WATCH OUT FOR MOTORCYCLES!"

It gave new meaning to that message. Even with their headlights on, motorcycles can be hard to notice, especially if drivers in four-wheeled vehicles are in a hurry.

My mind went to how often Jesus noticed people who were unseen, the marginalized in today's language. One day when he wanted to make a point with his apprentices, he called a child into the group. (Was it one of their children?) He not only noticed the child, but according to one account he held the little one in his arms while talking. In a society which valued children but didn't want them front and center, that was a bold move.

A century ago someone photographed a family in another culture. Mother, father, and children were all gussied up, posing carefully for their formal portrait. A missionary who knew that culture saw the photo and exclaimed, "That's a Christian family!" The obvious question was, "How do you know?" "It's simple," she said. "The father is holding the baby." That was unheard of before Christ.

Jesus consistently noticed the unnoticed, attending to those at the edges. The Gospel according to Luke in particular is aware of this. A Pharisee invited Jesus to dinner, but a woman crashed the party. In that society dinner for an honored guest could be an open-house affair. Any neighbor, especially a male, could enter and listen to the conversation with the visiting wise man. But this time a woman came in and stood behind Jesus as he reclined at the low table. She was weeping. Pouring perfume on his bare feet, she used her long hair to wipe off the mixture of tears, dust, and perfume.

The scene was scandalous, erotic. For a woman to let down her hair in public was a disgrace and valid cause for divorce. It was said that many a pious Jew died without ever seeing his wife's hair at its full length. Further, Jesus should have known what kind of woman this was. She was a "sinner," one who, for whatever reason, did not observe the rites and standards of the Pharisees. Perhaps worst of all, she was touching Jesus, and he allowed her to do so. The host's revulsion was palpable as he mentally accused Jesus. "That Nazarene is no holy man. He is no prophet. He is a corrupter of public morals!"

Jesus asked, "Simon, do you see this woman?" Of course, he saw her. Her image had registered on his retina and burned into his brain. But did he "see" her in the sense Jesus intended? No. He did not – he could not – allow such a "sinner" to come close, brush his spirit, and maybe touch his heart.

A few years ago a writer recounted a very special college experience. It was halfway through the course and time for the mid-term examination. The class was stunned when they read the test's opening question: "State the name of the person who cleans this classroom." The teacher later explained how important it is to notice those who may be unnoticed. Jesus would say, "Do you see, really see, this person?"

This is no command, no ought, or should, or must. It isn't one more duty added to our to-do list. We can't ask everyone's name, address, and Social Security number. But we can cultivate awareness. We can be attentive to the marginalized. We can notice the unnoticed. In truth, it is not we who see them – it is God looking at them through us.

Bill Hybels, founding pastor of the Willowcreek megachurch, believes we should not try to share our faith with everyone we meet. Rather, we should live so much in the Spirit, so closely tuned to Christ within, that we are sensitive to what Hybels calls God's promptings. Those nudges urge us into action, but can be resisted if we wish. On this view, the key to personal evangelism is not some sense of ought, or should, or must. The key is spiritual formation, and when the Spirit says, "Do you see this person?" we are ready to respond as Jesus would.

The late Henri Nouwen in his book *Reaching Out* told of a day when a former student stopped by his office. "I have no questions to ask," he said. "I need no advice. I'd just like to spend some time with you." Nouwen was always ready for such an experience, so they went outside. As they walked they discussed what had happened in the student's life since he graduated. Eventually they found a place where they could sit and continue talking. There was traffic noise nearby and the sound of a trash truck making its pickup, but that did not interfere.

As they spoke, their sentences slowed to a standstill and a comfortable silence began to enfold them. After a while the visitor said, "It's good to be here!" "Yes," replied Nouwen, "it's good to be together again." They smiled slightly at one another as the silence resumed. Some minutes later the guest spoke again: "When I see you, I feel I'm in the presence of Christ." Unfazed by such an expression, Nouwen replied, "It's the Christ in you who is able to see the Christ in me." They continued to sit in silence until the graduate finally said, "From now on, wherever I go or wherever you go, all the ground between us will be holy ground." Henri Nouwen later commented that on that day he learned the true meaning of Christian community.

"Do you see this person?" If you do, it's the Christ in you who is able to notice the unnoticed, to see the Christ in them. When this happens, all the ground between can indeed be truly holy.

Sometimes that may occur without any word from us. Several years ago I was standing in the checkout line at a local place of business. The largest young man I have ever seen was in front of me. Now, I've been hugged by a former NFL lineman, but this young fellow seemed even bigger. He was simply enormous, and likely unhealthy. He was wearing a tee shirt and shorts. His tree-trunk legs were wrapped in elastic bandages from the ankle all the way up. My heart went out to him. I began to wonder what challenges he had faced in life so far – not just physical but mental, emotional, spiritual, social challenges.

I hung back a little as he stepped up to the cashier. But he didn't seem to be doing any business. He and the lady behind the counter quietly exchanged a few words, but no money changed hands. Then as he turned to leave I heard him say in a clear voice, "Love you, mom." "I love you, son," she replied.

I stood transfixed. He wasn't just the largest young man I'd ever seen. He wasn't just a big guy with lots of problems. He was somebody's son, and I was about to meet his mother. I was standing on holy ground.

All the ground between us is holy ground when the Risen One is present. Jesus asked his mealtime host, "Do you see this woman?" Do you, can you, will you notice the unnoticed? We can, if we live so that it is Christ in us who does it. We can see with his eyes, hear with his ears, feel with his heart, and then act as he prompts.

So, please – watch out for motorcycles. Watch for people. Be alert for God. They all have a way of showing up.

23

A FRIEND TO SLAVES

I learned a new word not long ago – *degaje*. Traditionally it's been used in poverty-stricken Haiti for "making do with what you've got." It usually declares some sense of independence. But lately the meaning has become more sinister.

Degaje now refers to girls who "make do" by selling their bodies, young girls who voluntarily enter prostitution. It is the choice they make to stave off starvation. Sell your body in order to buy food or die without food – the choice is hideous.

It's one more example of the human trafficking that infects our world, in this instance especially evil because it is voluntary, not forced. And yet it is forced – forced by the ignorance, poverty, despotism, and war that choke so much of our beautiful planet. With one-third of Haiti's population under age fourteen, the situation is desperate.

It has always been desperate somewhere in the world. No time in history has been without human trafficking. But whether it is kidnapping to produce child soldiers, abduction into the sex industry, forced labor in factories, or "voluntary" *degaje* – buying and selling human beings like so much livestock is an abomination.

The Gospels mention various times when Jesus felt compassion (in Greek, a gut-wrenching sensation). In each instance he responded to address that wrenching need. He fed the multitudes, healed the sick, and "began to teach them many things." He restored a widow's son to life and lit up the darkened eyes of Bartimaeus. He wept at the tomb of Lazarus, and then went to work: "Lazarus, come out! . . . Unbind him, and let him go." He did not feed all of the world's hungry, heal all the sick, or raise all the dead. But he did what he could in each instance to bring life, love, and freedom from what enslaves.

As his followers, his pupils, we also weep at the world's suffering – we must weep. We also work, but not in a hasty, adolescent way which thinks we can cure all pain in a fortnight. Human trafficking is just one example of the suffering that calls for long-term many-sided solutions.

I described earlier how America's Quakers sent Dr. Thomas Kelly to Germany in 1938 before the Nazi government closed its borders to prepare for war. Upon his return Kelly wrote, "There is an inexorable amount of suffering in all life, blind, aching, unremovable, not new but only terribly intensified in these days. . . . But there is also removable suffering, yet such as yields only to years of toil and fatigue and unconquerable faith and perhaps to death itself."

He pled with his gentle, cultured Philadelphia friends to let their hearts be broken by the things that break the heart of God (as World Vision's founder Bob Pierce put it later). But, "we cannot die on *every* cross," said Kelly, "nor are we expected to." Rather, God parcels out the great bundle of world concerns, giving to each of us the portion we are to bear – "God's burdened heart particularizing His burdens in our hearts."

In painful sensitivity and persistent obedience we respond. It may be in programs that soar heavenward like skyscrapers. It may be in prayer that anchors their foundations in the Rock. But always the call is to persist, as it was for Thomas Clarkson and William Wilberforce. Both devout Christians, they strove together in Parliament more than forty long years to abolish human trafficking in the British Empire.

Wilberforce has become famous through biographies and the film "Amazing Grace." He is buried in Westminster Abbey, where a large statue marks his grave. It is the highest honor Great Britain can give. His friend Clarkson, who outlived him by a dozen years, is buried elsewhere, largely forgotten. But near the tomb of Wilberforce a simple memorial plaque reads, "Thomas Clarkson, 1760-1846. A Friend to Slaves."

Victims of slavery in today's world need more of such friends.

24

I DON'T GET ANYTHING OUT OF IT

How often have you heard, "I don't go to church because I don't get anything out of it"? The worship wars produce the cry "I don't get anything!" The multiple-choice options are almost without number. The place where we worship is too hot or too cold. The seating is too open or too cramped. The lights are too dim or too bright. The music is too loud or too soft, too slow or too fast, too traditional or too contemporary. The sermon is too stuffy or too slangy, too short or too long. Options and objections abound without number.

This reflects our culture where life revolves around "me, myself, and I." Individualism outranks community, personal preference replaces common good, and instant results downgrade delayed gratification. Fast food, quick service, and guaranteed satisfaction are the coin of the day. And when nothing seems to work out, shop around for a better deal.

Churches and their leaders, pastors and parishioners

are up against it. We will always worship something because we are hard-wired to admire. But we can wind up admiring style over substance and sizzle more than steak.

I don't get anything out of brushing my teeth twice a day. Every day. I get nothing out of having to shower and shave every day except that I'm clean. It's no great emotional experience – it's just what is good for health and hygiene.

And worship? It's not about me, it's about God. And I'm not there to get anything – I'm there to give God what is due. I'm there to say thanks for my blessings and join the family of faith in reaffirming our trust in the One who is source, savior, and sustainer of our life. I enjoy my friends. I enjoy complimenting them, telling them how much they mean to me. In worship I tell the Father, Son, and Spirit in song and scripture, in prayer and praise, how much they mean to me.

Yet I do get something out of it. I reconnect with others who are on the same team. We belong to this faith family, and together we pledge our allegiance. Long ago at Rice Elementary School I joined my classmates in reciting the pledge to the American flag every day. Every day. (This was long before the words "under God" were added.) I don't recall getting much out of that routine, but George always seemed to. George had freckles and a shock of brown hair. And when we recited the pledge, he seemed to light up. His face just glowed. Clearly, saying those words, no matter how many times, had significance for him. So it is possible to engage in routine and get something from it.

When I'm attentive I can get something, however faint, from a worship service. There's a story supposedly from the 19th century on just this point. An old lady (I'll call her Nell) kept going to church even though her mind was failing. Faithful spirit was present, but short-term memory was lacking. Sitting on her porch, she listened as several snarky boys began to tease her. By the time she returned home, they said, she couldn't remember any of the service. Especially the sermon. She could never recall any of the sermon. So why go?

Finally Nell stood up and went inside the house. She picked up her coal basket from beside the fireplace and took it outside. "Here, boys" she said to the rascals. "Take my basket down to the spring and bring me a basket of water."

Winking and nodding at one another, the boys headed down to the spring. Now they were sure the old woman was daft. Who could carry water in a basket? Still, they filled the coal basket from the spring and headed back up to Nell's house. Of course, by the time they got there, all the water had drained out of the basket.

When confronted with the damp, empty basket, Nell agreed that it was empty of water. "But," she said, "don't you see? Now my basket is cleaner than it was."

Ah, cleaner. When I join my sisters and brothers to focus together on the God of our lives, I can come away cleaner, refreshed, and maybe even inspired. I can get something out of worship even though that is not its goal. The goal of worship is the God of my life, the God of both grandeur and goodness.

The great evangelist D. L. Moody said that he needed multiple fillings of the Holy Spirit. When asked why he needed to be filled again and again, Moody's answer was classic: "Because I leak!" I leak too. I go to corporate worship to join with companions in the Way. Together we thank the God of our life and pledge our allegiance once more. I may not get a lot out of the experience every time, but in the process I return home cleaner than before. Whether I feel it or not, I did get something out of it.

25

THE WHOLE STORY IN FIVE WORDS

I once spent a month at a Catholic monastery. For a low-church Protestant, it was little short of radical. As a seminary professor I was allowed sabbatical leave, and since I was teaching spiritual formation, a monastery experience seemed appropriate. Facilities for extended stay were available, and I could attend monastic prayers in the large church as often as I wished. This Benedictine house also had an accredited seminary on the grounds, so there was opportunity to sit in on a class and do library research.

On arrival I learned I could have spiritual direction while I was there. The monk in charge of that suggested several of the brothers who might be available. I telephoned the first one, Father Keith, and made an appointment for the next day at his office. To my surprise, he was the monk I ate dinner with in the cafeteria the night before. He hadn't worn his robe that evening, just a shirt and slacks.

In the days that followed I began to experience a special call from God. I was overwhelmed at what I was sensing. It was a call to something that seemed too difficult for me. It was a summons beyond anything I had ever attempted. The impossible dream called up all my inability and unworthiness and fear.

Tears were close the following week as I told Father Keith about it. As monks often do, he suggested a scripture to pray with until our next appointment. It was the call of Moses in Exodus 3-4. That should be good, I thought. Moses' call had been the text of my first sermon at age eighteen. But I was in for a surprise.

At eighteen I had analyzed Exodus 3-4 in detail. I outlined and diagrammed, sliced and diced until I knew the passage forward and backward. I knew the steps in God's approach and all of Moses' excuses. And I preached the call of Moses, all his objections, and how this applies to us today.

But now I was sixty, trembling under the weight of God's hand. The call, the summons, was to service beyond my experience, beyond my abilities. Now God's call to Moses sounded different. I found something in the story I had missed years ago, or maybe now it rang in my ears with new awareness. "I am with you," God said. Despite Moses' sense of being unprepared, the assurance was the same. "I will be with you. I will give you words. I will give you a companion. I will not leave you." Again and again, "I am with you."

As I pondered Exodus and Moses and me, I reached a tentative conclusion. The message of the whole Bible, the story of our faith, might be distilled in the simple words "I am with you" or "I will be with you." I, wandering around in my confusion, am not alone. We befuddled bipeds whirling on this dust-speck in space are not alone. This is the visited planet, and I AM is here. That's what God told Moses, and that story threads all through the Bible.

When Moses approached the end of his days, God told him that his assistant, Joshua ben-Nun, was to succeed him. Joshua in turn received the same assurance God had given to Moses. "As I was with Moses, so I will be with you; I will not fail you or forsake you" (Josh. 1:5). His challenge was enormous – attack and capture fortified cities with an amateur army. Unrealistic. Over the top. Insane. But there it was, "for the Lord your God is with you wherever you go."

Centuries later, when Israel was threatened by hostile kings, the same message came to the prophet Isaiah. A child would be born and named Immanuel; that is, "God with us" (Isa. 7:14). Not long after his birth the menacing kings would disappear. Still later the same message came to Israel in spiritual or physical exile.

> *Do not fear, for I have redeemed you;*
> *I have called you by name, you are mine.*
> *When you pass through the waters, I will be with you;*
> *and through the rivers, they shall not overwhelm you . . . .*
> *Do not fear, for I am with you.*
> *(Isaiah 43:2-3, 5)*

That call challenged Judah to leave exile and return home. Still later, such lines, taken as Christian experience, found their way into successive stanzas of the great anonymous hymn "How Firm a Foundation."

Matthew's Gospel begins and ends with the words "I am with you." First, it describes the birth of Jesus as fulfilling Isaiah's Immanuel promise. Then, after recounting Jesus' life and work, his death and resurrection, it concludes by reporting that he said, "I am with you always, to the end of the age." For two thousand years his followers have clung, sometimes desperately, to that assurance. Missionaries, martyrs, and countless regular folks have bet their lives on the truth of that promise.

The most dramatic of Jesus' early followers was no doubt the apostle Paul. Whether at liberty or in lockup, he too affirmed the promise that I AM in the Spirit of Jesus is here and active. The book of Acts reports that in Corinth Paul received the assurance "Do not be afraid, . . . for I am with you" (18:9-10). The result was one of his longest periods of activity in one place. But the chaotic Corinthians gave Paul trouble, so he later wrote to them his most personal letter. It concludes with these words: "Put things in order, listen to my appeal, agree with one another, live in peace, and the God of peace will be with you" (2 Cor. 13:11).

There are other biblical instances in which God promised divine presence and protection, provision and peace in the same words – "I am with you" or "I will be with you." From their first mention to Jacob when he fled his brother's murderous threats (Gen. 28:15) to John's vision of the new Jerusalem (Rev. 21:3), the message is the same. The whole story is in five words.

Father Keith was right. When facing a challenge or wrestling with a call, return to Moses, Joshua & Company. Pray with them. Let the assurance given to them become your own. It's not a guarantee of painless performance, but of divine companionship. When the skies are dark and the danger is grave, I AM promises to be there, not to extract you from the situation, but to be with you in it. That's why on the cross Jesus could pray, "My God, my God, why?" and then later, "Father, into your hands I commend my spirit." Faith in the fact of Abba's presence has the last word.

26

IN THE HALL OF THE NURSING HOME

Sequined with diamonds, the snow drapes in the noonday sun like a bridal gown. Quietly I walk amid the traffic to the mansion where once a wealthy family had its life. Now its halls are home to some for whom it is the last stopping place.

Into the building, saying hello to nurses and aides. We're friends now as I come and go. Talk with the nurse about Mother's condition. "She's walking in the hall," Becky says.

In the distance I spy her: frail, stooped, ninety-two years borne in her body. I come alongside, slip my arm lightly around her small shoulders. "Hello, mother. . . . Hello, mother. . . . Mother, it's me, Jerry. . . ." I speak the words much, much slower than they can be read. "Would you like to sit down? . . . How nice you look today. . . . I like your striped red blouse. You must like it too. . . . I love you. . . ."

The silence is hard, but not unexpected. The slow,

slow monologue continues. I stroke her back as we sit together and gently hold her close to me.

At last she speaks. Random words, non-words, a short quilt of sounds stitched together with no discernible pattern. Syllables without words. Words without meaning. Speech without communication. If there is structure, I cannot find it. If there is meaning, I cannot share it. Memory is gone, meaning is gone. And the one-way conversation is ended.

Walking back amid humming traffic and bridal snow, I am lost in my own inner world. When I was too young to speak to her, she was there with me. Even now she is here in me, and something of me resides in her as well.

Immanuel – God with us in Advent. Calvary – God for us in Lent. Pentecost – God in us until now. God with me, God for me, God in me. So I am content to be with her, and for her, and somehow in her until she sleeps.

God hold her close, keep her safe, and take her Home.

27

LAST DAYS

The concentrator huffs in the corner,
puffing breath through its plastic tube
to his wasted body in the bed.
Silent he lies,
veteran of ninety-four years,
tiny form fetus-like on the pillow.

Nurses and aides come and go softly.
He knows them all, and they love him.
Some return off duty to give a meal
or cry or just to sit with him.
I catch their rhythm, the pace of last days,
and learn to walk with them.

No outsiders, he insists – no TV, talk or music.
Only silence as he thinks long thoughts
toward the inevitable.

"Hi," he whispers. "Why are we here?"
Eyelids close.
No discussion needed.

Time to leave. I begin to read,
hoping he will fall asleep
to the warming of the words.

"The Lord is my shepherd;
I shall not want. . . .
Though I walk through the valley
of the shadow of death . . .
I will dwell in the house of the Lord
for ever."

He is still awake. I begin again:
"The Lord is my shepherd. . . ."
Quiet he lies, eyes now closed.
Then he speaks once more:
"When you say the first line,
You've said it all.
'The Lord, Yahweh, my shepherd.'
"That's all any sheep needs."

I kiss his forehead, close the door,
and walk outside under the stars.
First word is last word:
You, Lord, my shepherd. . . .
Selah. Amen. Indeed.

28

BENEDICTION

Go now with the living God,
who moves before you to prepare the way.
And as you go . . .

May God's Joy be the joy of your morning,
for the Lord takes delight in your very existence.

May God's Love be your strength
through the long hours of the day.

May God's Peace be your portion
as you rest at evening.

And may God's Grace, which has brought you safe thus far,
prevail to lead you Home.

Through Jesus Christ our Lord. Amen.

ABOUT THE AUTHOR

Since the age of eight when he first walked his church's red-carpeted aisle for salvation, Jerry Flora has been a Jesus follower. Answering a call to ministry, he trained at the former Ashland College and Seminary. He served as a pastor first in a small village in Indiana and then in an urban neighborhood in Washington, D.C. Graduate degrees from Fuller Seminary and The Southern Baptist Theological Seminary readied him for a teaching career. He returned to Ashland Seminary where he taught for thirty years. At retirement in 2002 Dr. Flora was named Professor Emeritus of Theology and Spiritual Formation.

Although he has lived from coast to coast, he is a Hoosier by birth and a Buckeye by adoption. Along the way he has been a janitor, caddy, lawn-care worker, choir director and retreat speaker. He was co-founder of the LifeSpring School of Spiritual Formation and its co-director for ten years. From 1995 to 2008 he was a guest instructor at Pennsylvania's Kairos School of Spiritual Formation. He has also served as national vice-president and newsletter editor for the Disciplined Order of Christ.

Dr. Flora and his wife Julie have been married almost sixty years. They have two daughters, Janet and Ann, and two grandchildren, Vanessa and Matthew. A soul-friend to many, he relishes family and friends, reading and music, sunrise and sunset.

Made in the USA
Charleston, SC
20 October 2015